Praise for the Original
ESSAYS THAT WORKED

"Outstanding."
The Journal of College Admissions

"For inspiration on what makes a memorable
essay, read *Essays That Worked*."
Money Magazine

"The best sort of teaching tool."
School Library Journal

"The collection reveals as much about the sorts of
students who are applying to college as about
the application process itself."
The Chronicle of Higher Education

Also published by Ballantine Books

ESSAYS THAT WORKED *for* **COLLEGE APPLICATIONS:**
*50 Essays that Helped Students Get Into
the Nation's Top Colleges*

ESSAYS THAT WORKED *for* **BUSINESS SCHOOLS:**
*40 Essays from Successful Applications
to the Nation's Top Business Schools*

ESSAYS THAT WORKED *for* **MEDICAL SCHOOLS:**
*40 Essays from Successful Applications
to the Nation's Top Medical Schools*

ESSAYS *That* WORKED®
for LAW SCHOOLS

*40 Essays from Successful Applications
to the Nation's Top Law Schools*

REVISED AND UPDATED

Edited by BOYKIN CURRY *and* EMILY ANGEL BAER

www.essaysthatworked.com

BALLANTINE BOOKS • NEW YORK

For Rollin Riggs, who with patience, humor, hard work,
and entrepreneurial spirit, gives life to ideas.

And for Dennis R. Baer and Isadore B. Baer
for showing what lawyers should be.

ACKNOWLEDGMENTS

This book was created with the help of many students and admissions officers at some of the top law schools in America. We deeply appreciate the generosity of the applicants who let us reprint their essays and of the admissions officers who gave us their time, critiques, and advice.

We wish to extend our gratitude to several people in particular: Debbie Land, Christina Benet, Jean Webb, Kent Frandsen, and Marge Roosa. All went far beyond their duties and gave us invaluable assistance.

CONTENTS

ESSAYS *That* WORKED
for LAW SCHOOLS

INTRODUCTION

How important is the essay on a law school application? Along with your grades, your accomplishments, and, in some cases, your LSAT scores, your application essay can determine whether you are accepted or rejected. For some law schools, the essay is crucial: a great essay can make admissions officers discount poor grades or scores; a bad essay can ruin an otherwise sterling application. For other schools, the essay is considered seriously only on borderline candidates and is used only to "tip the scales."

It all depends on the school. One admissions officer told us flatly, "We do not use the essay as a major factor." Another officer said, "The essay is not going to vault someone to the top of the pack from the middle, but it can be determinative for some middle-of-the-road applicants. And it is more important than that for minority applicants."

Said still another: "It is a vital element of our admissions policy."

After speaking with admissions officers at a variety of law schools, we tried to estimate just how important the essay can be in the admissions process. The following graph illustrates roughly the relative importance of the essay at these schools:

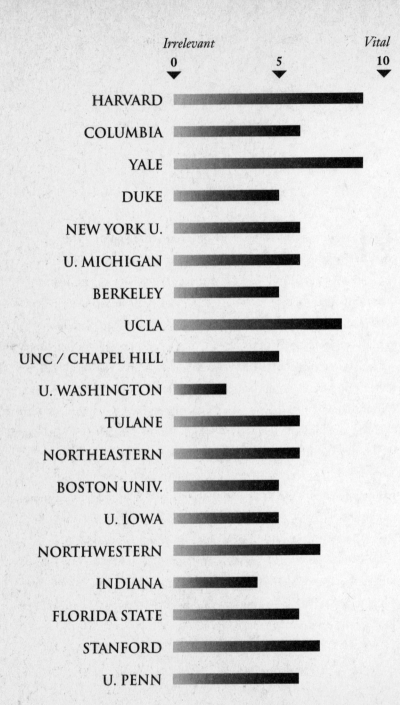

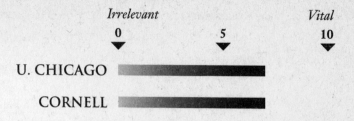

In our previous books on college and business school application essays, we discussed what kinds of content and tone were most appropriate. Much of our earlier advice holds true for law school applications as well.

Overwhelmingly, admissions officers everywhere complain about the same thing: reading 13,000 essays on the same few topics in just three months is a mind-numbing experience. Most essays are dry and overwritten. They are often "corrected" by so many friends and relatives that the life gets sucked out. One undergraduate admissions officer noted that "few applicants understand what we want to read, and they rarely go out on a limb to be witty or controversial." Anxious applicants become so afraid of saying the wrong thing that they say nothing at all. Such sterilization can mean unbearable monotony for the hapless reader, so don't treat your essay like a psychological mine-field. What seems "safe" to you may be deadly boring to a weary admissions officer.

The officer at one top business school resorted to dramatic measures to combat essay fatigue. "I try to change the scenery when I read essays," he said. "I read them in the park or out on my boat. You know what? Even that doesn't help."

Now imagine that same cynical admissions officer finding your lively, original essay in the middle of the pile. For starters, your application is *noticed*—and most likely remembered—and that is much of the battle. Plus, you have done a favor for the tired reader. Favors are often returned.

"I've noticed that law faculty who are on admissions committees typically want to know why the candidate wants to go to law school," one Dean of Admissions said wearily. "I don't much care about that. I just want an essay that grabs me."

A piece doesn't have to be a hilarious comedy or a literary jewel to "grab" the reader. Something simple, honest, and sincere can be more disarming than sophisticated humor or strategic pledges to work for worldwide justice.

The buzzword among admissions officers these days is "authenticity," but it describes what admissions officers will always want: some kind of proof that you are a lively, sensitive, bright person with whom they can *identify*.

After reading the essays in this book, we hope you will understand better the boundaries of tone and content within which you can work, and we hope you see how large those boundaries are. Some of the essays are written masterfully. Some are a little clumsy, and some are, frankly, rather dull. But, in the opinion of the admissions officer who sent it to us, each essay "worked." Why? Because it revealed a part of the applicant's personality that wasn't shown in grades and LSAT scores. Each writer took the opportunity to convert a large chunk of fearsome blank paper into a personal message to the admissions staff. And that's the whole point of the exercise.

Since these essays represent some of the best out of thousands submitted each year, they should serve to inspire your creativity and help you feel more comfortable about the admissions process. As the essays demonstrate, you can be exciting and natural without resorting to outrageous gimmicks or immature poses. And you don't have to be Ernest Hemingway—or even an English major—to write an effective personal statement. An honest, enthusiastic reflection of your personality can make for a refreshing—and we hope successful—essay. Good luck!

AN INTERVIEW *with*
an ADMISSIONS OFFICER

Although different schools attach different levels of importance to the application essays, and although each school may be looking for a slightly different type of student, admissions officers have surprisingly similar desires. They want brevity. They want sincerity. They want mature enthusiasm. And a little humor—when it's truly humorous—doesn't hurt.

But as we pondered the application question and tried to compose our own "personal statement," we found ourselves asking a number of questions. How "lawyer-like" should we be? How much can we joke around? Can we relax and be the readers' chum, or should we treat them as clients? Should we tell them what we think they want to hear, or should we be totally honest, even at the risk of being dull?

We asked these and other questions to dozens of admissions officers at almost every major law school in the country. The following is a condensed version of those interviews, along with relevant comments from admissions people whom we interviewed earlier at business schools and colleges:

What's the difference between application essays for law school and the essays we wrote to get into college?

The main difference is the way the author presents himself. What we ask of a college graduate is much more difficult than what colleges ask of a high school senior. And it should be. We don't want applicants to simply give a self-absorbed description of themselves, as they did for their college application. Rather, we want them to describe the world they see around them and their place in it. An analogy we like to use around here is that with the essay, a student fashions a lens for us to view the world. From looking at the quality of that lens, we hope to judge the quality of its maker.

We also expect more maturity for law school. That's partly a function of age but it's also an issue of direction. Undergraduates are coming to school to explore. It's hard to justify giving one of a few spots to someone who is not pretty committed to a law career.

I used your undergraduate book for a talk I gave on the application essay, but I had to warn everyone that this is not high school any more. Some of the essays in your first book would have been fine, but others are way too cutesy for us. Essays about socks and pets and Oreos [*Essays That Worked for College Applications*] would be a real detriment to a law school application.

Do you want a description of a person or just a prose listing of accomplishments?

We want an essay that brings the whole set of numbers into a coherent form. We want inconsistencies explained, and we want to see diverse activities as different facets of a single personality. We'd like to be able to say, "Oh, he did that, yeah, that makes sense. That fits with what we have." Both the performer and his track record should be discussed, so that we can know the person underneath all the accomplishments, and also how those activities affected that person.

Nine times out of ten, people who write a really good personal statement don't have the supporting facts to back it up. A student will say he wants to be a lawyer to stop racial injustice, but then he'll write an essay about "learning to scuba dive helped me overcome my fear of water" or something. Tell me about your legal aid work, or your work in the Big Brother program, or something like that. Inconsistency knocks an applicant down quite a few pegs in my judgment.

Are there any hackneyed topics that applicants should avoid?

"Why I want to be a public defender . . ." or "I have always wanted to be a lawyer since I was ten. My daddy was a lawyer and he took me to court and I enjoyed it . . ." I mean, who cares? Do they really expect us to think some kind of immaculate revelation hit them at age ten? It makes me wonder if they have thought carefully about the decision they are making.

It may sound insensitive, but a common essay that almost never works is about "my mother's death" or "my medical history." They're almost always manipulative, and they rarely come to important conclusions. If such an incident truly reveals your character, fine, but we're looking for much more than just another hard-luck story.

"What I think about justice" is also far too common. Since we are a law school, I suppose it's to be expected, but so many people do it that you have to write a very good essay to stand out. Also, since we know the law and the students have not yet studied it, essays on the law risk sounding naive and ill-informed. I'm not saying an applicant should avoid this topic; just don't jump straight to it.

Of course, then someone starts up, "Since I was ten . . ." and bursts into something truly wonderful. Really, the similarity in topics is not what makes essays dull—and most of them certainly are. It's the monotonous style. Applicants tend to use too many big words and amorphous adjectives and not enough colorful details and observations.

The first 50 essays that come in are okay, but by 3,575 we start to look at them very quickly—and they'd better have something interesting to say.

If reading essays is so boring, would you prefer that applicants try to entertain you?

It's not their job to do that, and the applicants who are accepted tend not to have massive entertainment value. We also read no more than 20 essays at a sitting, so that shock value doesn't take on overriding importance. Still, I do confess to some weakness for catchy or clever turns.

Nothing is worse than something that seems unnatural, though—and gimmicks do not work. One year we got an essay written in crayon on construction paper. It really hurt the applicant because it made us question his maturity and competence. That kind of joking might work occasionally for a college application, but we are dealing with much more sophisticated people at this level. Jokers are admitted only if their credentials are so good that we just can't refuse them.

You do have to captivate the reader somewhat, but many people hurt themselves by going too far. One applicant wrote an eight-page essay when we asked for one page. She was entertaining, but she didn't arrive at any point. And she didn't get very far in the admissions process, either.

Being offbeat just to get attention won't work. The uniqueness has to mesh with the rest of the application. We do want to see different facets of an applicant's personality. We do want people to show us how they differ from the other 7,000 applicants. But different doesn't mean outrageous. It can mean a paralegal who takes ghetto kids camping on weekends, or a math major with a passion for billiards. It does not mean some goofball just trying to impress us with a bunch of one-liners.

Some applicants have sent videotapes and put ads in the newspaper here. Unless it shows some relevant skill in a very meaningful way, a display like that is a waste of time.

I suppose my best advice is to write a mature essay—nothing too formal, though—and to integrate your personality into it as best you can. Don't be afraid to say what you feel. Remember that serious is not synonymous with humorless. We love wit, but it also has to be backed up with meaningful points.

Is motivation important? Do you want to see what an applicant plans to do with the degree?

Motivation can be important, but it must be explained and supported. Everyone talks about wanting to help people. Why? What motivates you, specifically?

From what I read, you would think everyone is going into *pro bono* work as soon as they graduate. Of course, we know that won't happen. We are sensitive to the fact that many essays may be contrived to what the applicant thinks are the committee's priorities. Since an undergraduate has no real notion of all the options available in the legal profession, an essay about "here's the kind of law I plan to be practicing in 20 years" is really not very valuable.

Do you want a good writer or a good person?

Both, of course. A vote on that might divide our committee 3-3, but I think writing quality may edge out the limited insight we can glean from a 300-word essay. Expressing yourself is a key part of the profession, after all. You may never have to argue a case in court, but you'll always have to write. We want to know about you, but behind that is whether you can deal with the language and communicate.

Good writers are convincing and engaging. They know how to intrigue an audience, and they back up their points with specific, relevant details. Their ideas flow smoothly, and they make the reader's job a lot easier. And if they are intelligent and witty, the essay is hard to forget.

One applicant wrote an essay wondering why people on death row always ask for a cigarette instead of writing down something about their lives or even making a last statement. Well, it is incredibly hard to express yourself, and we know that, so don't let your anxiety about style interfere with your need to write a meaningful essay.

There'd better be no typos, though—it's amazing how many we get. We are always getting letters two weeks after receiving an essay apologizing for mistakes. Lots of times they enclose a "revised copy." Well, if they care so much about getting into our law school, why didn't they read over the essay before they sent it? I don't want to be distracted by grammar mistakes and organizational problems. There is no excuse for not having your essay reviewed by friends or a teacher. It should be polished.

The essay isn't the only view we get of your articulation skills. We get writing on your LSAT writing sample, too. The essay shows us what an applicant can do in a longer period of time, of course, but sometimes we wonder if the essay and the writing sample could possibly have been written by the same person.

So what are you looking for?

Truthfully, we don't have a set agenda. We don't know what we're looking for until we read it.

I want to know who the applicant is and why she wants to go to law school. How she thinks. Or what she cares about. Sometimes I've been in tears by the end of an essay. Occasionally one will make me laugh for the rest of the day. But most successful essays need not be dramatic. We want people to be vibrant, but we don't want gimmicks. We want a mature approach, but we don't want to be fed dull, pompous lines.

I want an honest, thoughtful essay. I know that sounds a little trite, but it's something we rarely see. Not only is that the best essay to read, but it should be the easiest to write. Concocting ridiculous anecdotes, attention-getting schemes, or a fictitious portrait is really a big waste of time and energy.

Everyone wants us to give a recipe and a road map to the admissions process, but what we want is someone who can navigate his own course. Within guidelines, of course.

THE BASIC ESSAY QUESTION

We found the following essay question on a recent application to an Ivy League law school. While the question varies somewhat from school to school, this is basically what you can expect:

You may wish to submit a statement or essay supplementing required application materials, which would provide the Admissions Committee with information regarding such matters as personal, family, or educational background, experiences and talents of special interest, one's reasons for applying to law school as they may relate to personal goals and professional expectations, or any other factors that you think should inform the Committee's evaluation of your candidacy for admission. Such a statement should be submitted with the application materials.

However, most law school applications don't even give you that much. The most common "question" we found was a simple line that said *Personal Statement*, followed by a fearsome blank space, leaving content and direction wide open. At the other extreme, one school offered this as a topic:

"Restriction of free thought and free speech is the most dangerous of all subversions. It is the one un-American act that could easily defeat us."

*—William O. Dougla*s

Respond.

Regardless of the topic, there are a few essential ingredients to a successful essay. First, the introduction must be compelling; it's the most important part. A good first impression makes the reader want to keep reading.

Second, because most applications officers spend six to eight minutes evaluating your essay, you need a strong finish—one they will remember.

If you accomplish these two tasks, the reader is going to pay more attention to your essay—and that's good news and bad news. The bad news: He'll be more likely to find errors or typos (of which there should be none). The good news: You've got a great opportunity to make a personal connection with someone deciding your law school fate.

One law school admissions officer noted that dull, unmotivated personal statements work directly against the applicant. A bad personal statement can indicate a cavalier attitude, and even applicants with high LSAT scores and high GPAs have been denied because of a bad essay.

The University of Kentucky College of Law has one of the best Web sites we've seen, with straightforward advice about the personal statement that's appropriate for any application. Some of the points are:

Writing skills are the key to success as a law student. Your readers will expect a well-edited, well-composed essay.

While you'll probably write your essay in the first person, avoid starting every sentence with "I." Your reader is most likely a fifty-year-old law professor who is not amused by gimmicks. Don't use any. He or she will be more impressed by strong, declarative sentences, well-structured paragraphs, and an interesting topic.

But that's not to say that your essay should be lifeless. Remember, you're trying to stand out in a positive sense.

Finally, if you have a choice of questions, go for the one that best suits you and the school to which you're applying. All law schools are not alike. When you applied to undergraduate universities, you may have written one essay and used it on eight applications. For law school, expect to write several essays. Yes, it's a lot more work, but if you're a borderline student, a unique essay that addresses the individual school can make a big difference in the admission decision.

For more, see www.uky.edu/Law/admissions/pers_st.htm.

USING—*and* ABUSING—*the* INTERNET

The admissions officer is sitting at his desk, piles of papers everywhere indicating the degree to which he is overworked (or perhaps his own relaxed approach to organization). He is reading the forty-ninth essay of the day, when suddenly he has a wave of déjà vu.

Now, he's been reading admissions essays at his private law school for five years, and he's often read essays that remind him of something else. But this one—hmmmm:

New Albany City, check. Time, 15:30. Great! Reset timer; power normal; oil temperature, within range; compass setting, correct. Alone at 4,000 feet in a small airplane in a strange new territory and I am piloting my way perfectly. I feel like Lindbergh!

Is it possible that he's read about two student pilots this year? Coincidence? He thinks not. He reads through the essay about this young man's euphoric first solo flight and becomes more convinced that he has seen it before. He shuffles through the applications that he placed in a stack for a second review.

Bingo! There it is—the same essay in an application from two weeks ago. Punctuation, paragraphing, wording, all exactly the same. He glances through the application. One counselor recommendation

15

mentions the flying lessons; the other one does not. Both applicants come from large urban areas, but not the same urban area—not even the same state. Both are bright students and quite tech savvy. Their undergraduate transcripts and their extracurriculars indicate a big interest in the Internet. In fact, one teacher recommendation names the computer as the culprit when her student misses deadlines or comes to class unprepared. She intended to praise his expertise, but now the admissions officer is reading between the lines.

Taking a welcome break, he begins to surf the net himself and quickly finds several Web sites that offer help for grad school application essays. He subscribes to a few of the larger sites and finds one that will provide an essay of your choice on a variety of topics—for a fee, naturally. Thirty minutes later, he finds the exact essay the applicants submitted.

Both students are quickly rejected, of course. Furthermore, the admissions officer "unofficially" alerts his colleagues at the other colleges indicated on the students' LSAT reports. It seems unlikely that either student will attend the law school of his choice.

While this example is a compilation of several stories, the tale of the duplicate essay is absolutely true. Any dishonesty in connection with the application will prevent your admission to law school. If cheating is discovered after you've been accepted (and in one incident at Stanford, after a student had started classes), your acceptance will be rescinded.

While blatant plagiarism is rare, "canned" essays are becoming common. Increasingly, admissions officers are seeing the "packaging" of applicants. What has made this unhappy trend grow is the use—and abuse—of the Internet.

In one random search, we found almost a thousand Web sites "guaranteeing" a winning application essay—college, law school, business school, dental school, you name it. One service offers a "final polish of the essay." This same site adds: "Unlike other sites, our editors do not merely write a critique of your essay; instead, they actually correct and make changes to your essay while maintaining your unique voice." This claim is, by definition, impossible; if your voice is unique, how can "they" duplicate it? "They" don't even know you!

Another service is even more blatant. Their Web site states: "We draft your university, graduate, or professional school essays or college admissions statements from the information you provide to us." Another one simply asks for your bio, and they take it from there. Be aware that, while admissions readers are looking for your own voice, they're also pretty good at detecting when it's not there. They want to see how you express yourself. As one admissions director said, "When that expression becomes a product of someone else's work, there's a word for that: *plagiarism*."

The price for a graduate school application essay starts at $500, depending on how much assistance you receive and how fast you want it. The sites generally tout readers from schools such as Harvard, Yale, and Stanford, though there's no way to prove they have any affiliation with those schools—and chances are, they don't. Other sites are run by independent counselors (in one case, a mother who honestly admits she's just selling advice from her home) who charge fees for services that are provided free at most colleges and on many legitimate Web sites.

While many sites are perfectly honest, the Internet has provided almost unlimited possibilities for fraud. But you'll find that it's hard to deceive a good admissions officer. They've been trained; they've read hundreds of essays before yours; and they know at least as much about the Web as you do.

In fact, several Web sites, such as Plagiarized.com, help readers determine whether an essay is genuine, and there's software available specifically for detecting copied papers. Is it foolproof? Of course not. But is buying an essay off the Web a risk worth taking? Aside from the immorality of it, look at the practical aspect: If you submit a bad essay, it alone probably won't get you rejected. If you submit a plagiarized essay and it's discovered, you're immediately rejected—at that school, and probably at every school to which you've applied.

Of course, cheating is not new, and it won't disappear. The Internet simply offers enticing new ways to lure even the best students into thinking they need an essay service, when, in reality, it's the last thing they need. None of the essays in this book are Pulitzer Prize winners, but they are honest products of the students. When an essay isn't genuine, an admissions officer can smell it, and the results can be disastrous. And no one, no matter how desirable, is immune to close scrutiny on the essay. An admissions officer at Stanford recently said, "We just turned down an incredible prospect; the essays killed him." He went on to say that Stanford is seeing too much "editing" on student essays—sometimes the result of an overzealous school counselor, more often due to the growing influence of Internet sources.

An admissions officer from a private school in Georgia wrote:

I had a case this year of a kid who stole an essay off the Internet and tried to pass it off as his own. It sounded familiar but I couldn't put my finger on it. I posted something on the NACAC [National Association for College Admissions Counseling] website and within ten minutes people had sent me five or six sources. . . . By the way, I wrote a deny letter to him and sent a duplicate to his parents.

The Internet can provide terrific, legitimate suggestions and tips for all aspects of the application process, including the essay. The best place to start is at the law school's site itself. You can access any graduate school online by using the university's name, generally followed by ".edu." Read as much about the university as you can, including the questions they ask on their application. Familiarize yourself with whatever is unique about a specific institution. Ask yourself, "Why do I want to go to Takemeplease School of Law?" If you can answer that question, you can probably write a good essay.

Many Web sites are excellent sources for all kinds of university and admissions data. For example, www.collegeboard.com (associated with the College Board, which is more than a hundred years old) has useful information about all aspects of the process, including preparing for the LSAT, applying on-line, writing the essay, getting financial aid, and even choosing the school that's right for you.

The National Association for College Admissions Counseling (www.nacac.com) has great advice and links to other information sources, including essay help. Yahoo! offers several free services, some of which you must register for, such as LSAT tips and preparation, on-line applications, college searches, and financial aid.

The bottom line: Almost any information you want is available free on the Internet. But be careful, because the Internet alone can't get you through the application process. Not everything you see on the Internet is valid or germane to your experience.

According to the NACAC, more students are applying on-line every year. Critics say that some schools encourage on-line applications just to increase the number of applications they receive. This way, their well-publicized rejection rates will seem higher. Whether or not this is the case, it is a fact that the majority of universities today provide admission applications on-line. Some even have applications available on-line *only*. Remember that all electronic resources begin with what you yourself contribute. There is still no substitute for self-discovery. What motivates you in your choice of law schools: Location? Reputation? Accessible professors? Class size? Career guidance? What is significant about the particular school you wish to attend? How does it seem right for you? The more you know about yourself, the more useful on-line information can be.

One senior admissions officer wrote: "As students become increasingly Internet savvy, I think we will be experiencing a rise in those who are willing to apply on-line." As on-line applications increase, there will be more access to on-line aids—both honest and dishonest—for the application essays. The trick is to recognize the difference between helpful hints and outright cheating. Make your essay authentic. To be authentic, you should not sound like a forty-year-old editor. Your own voice is your best chance of showing an admissions officer that you are special and that you belong at his or her school.

Most of the on-line services for graduate school essays charge a fee, but these sites often provide very helpful hints in their free material. The following is an excellent "Do's and Don'ts" list from Accepted.com:

The Do's

- Unite your essay and give it direction with a theme or thesis. The thesis is the main point you want to communicate.

- Before you begin writing, choose what you want to discuss and the order in which you want to discuss it.

- Use concrete examples from your life experience to support your thesis and distinguish yourself from other applicants.

- Write about what interests you, excites you. That's what the admissions staff wants to read.

- Start your essay with an attention-grabbing lead—an anecdote, quote, question, or engaging description of a scene.

- End your essay with a conclusion that refers back to the lead and re-states your thesis.

- Revise your essay at least three times.

- In addition to your editing, ask someone else to critique your personal statement for you.

- Proofread your personal statement by reading it out loud or reading it into a tape recorder and playing back the tape.

- Write clearly, succinctly.

The Don'ts

- Don't include information that doesn't support your thesis.

- Don't start your essay with "I was born in . . . ," or "My parents came from. . . ."

- Don't write an autobiography, itinerary, or résumé in prose.

- Don't try to be a clown (but gentle humor is OK).

- Don't be afraid to start over if the essay just isn't working or doesn't answer the essay question.

- Don't try to impress your reader with your vocabulary.

- Don't rely exclusively on your computer to check your spelling.

- Don't provide a collection of generic statements and platitudes.

- Don't give mealymouthed, weak excuses for your GPA or test scores.

- Don't make things up.

There are other helpful Web sites as well. The following list can give you great advice and food for thought as you prepare to write your law school personal statement. Check them out, but use judiciously (pun intended):

The American Bar Association: www.abanet.org

Association of American Law Schools: www.aals.org

Boston College Online Law School Locator:
  www.bc.edu/bc_org/svp/carct/matrix.html#the25

Columbia Office of Pre-professional Programs per Web site
www.studentaffairs.columbia.edu/preprofessional

Columbia Law School: www.law.columbia.edu

Law School Application Essays: www.accepted.com/law

Index of Internet Legal Resources: www.findlaw.com

Thomas E. Brennan's *Judging the Law Schools*:
  www.ilrg.com/rankings

Law School Admission Council: www.lsac.org

Prelaw Handbook:
  oncampus.richmond.edu/academics/as/polsci/prelaw

Princeton Review Law section: www.review.com/law/index.cfm

Stanley Kaplan Law section:
  www.kaptest.com/repository/templates/Lev2InitDroplet
  .jhtml?_lev2Parent=/www/KapTest/docs/repository/content/Law

Peterson's—the Law Channel: www.petersons.com/law

Martindale-Hubbell Lawyer Directory: www.martindale.com

U.S. News & World Report Information and Rankings:
  www.usnews.com/usnews/edu/grad/rankings/law/
  lawindex_brief.php

The Internet is an enticing tool. But there's no substitute for simply reading real essays from real people. Take a hint from the examples collected here: Be yourself, whatever that may be. You're a college graduate, maybe you've already worked, maybe you already have a family, and your specific goal is to become a lawyer. Lawyer jokes aside, you have chosen to enter an honorable profession. Take a risk. Let your essay show your potential for growth, for contemplating new ideas, for change. Above all, be honest—to yourself, to your potential law school, and to your own future.

THE ESSAYS

For organizational purposes only, we divided the essays into seven groups. We created the introductions to each group of essays from the comments submitted by law school admissions officers and other admissions counselors. Please bear in mind that this grouping is totally artificial. You don't need to write an essay that would fit neatly into one of these categories.

As well as being a fine piece of writing, an essay might also exemplify a "type." For instance, the piece on the death of Michael Stewart (page 104) is a good example of an essay on injustice, which is a popular topic. So if you are planning to write this type of essay, pay special attention to the comments in the group's introduction, as well as to the actual essay.

Of course, the essay question may limit your range of responses. Most law schools ask for something vague and open-ended, such as "Please write something that will tell us more about you." For that, you could write about practically anything. Other schools have more specific topics that require much more focused writing.

The essays are reproduced almost exactly as they were submitted, though of course the fonts and spacing are different. We did not correct the writers' punctuation, spelling, or grammar—but note that very rarely would such correction be needed.

Since the authors of several essays requested anonymity, we occasionally deleted proper names and substituted a general name or date for a specific reference. In addition, at the request of a few schools, we sometimes disguised the name of the school to which the writer applied. However, our substitutions never distort the intent of the author.

Read Them All

Let's get one thing straight: The essays in this book are not standards that you have to meet in order to get into law school. Some of you might have essays in your head far better than anything here. (If so, let us read them! See **www.essaysthatworked.com** for information on submitting your essays for the next edition of this book.) These are simply essays that worked—not the *only* essays that worked.

We hope that you will first read all the essays. There's a wide range here; some are 500 words, some are 5,000. Some have dialogue, some are aggressive, some are reflective. The question you should ask yourself as you read is not, *Is this a good essay?* but rather, *Do I get to know this writer from this essay?* If you are an admissions officer, you will also ask, *Now that I know this applicant, does he/she match my law school?*

Getting into law school is not a writing contest; the competition is more subtle than that. More important than how well you write is how well you illustrate who you are and whether a particular school is right for you. Believe it or not, the admissions officer wants what's best for you. With the ever-increasing quality of the applicant pool, most schools have little trouble filling their first-year classes. Your task is to communicate something new and meaningful about yourself to someone who knows you only by your numbers.

A Warning

While we know that no one would be foolish enough to copy any of these essays verbatim, some of you might be tempted to take an essay and "change it around a little" to suit your application. We hope you know how stupid that would be. For one thing, stealing a phrase or even an idea from an essay in this book is flat-out dishonest. Duke University, the University of Virginia, and many other schools maintain that the application is covered by their Honor Codes. Thus, cheating on the application will guarantee your rejection from those schools. In fact, Stanford recently expelled a student two months into the academic year when they discovered he had plagiarized his application essay.

Remember, this has been a popular book for many years. Most admissions officers have read this book and are familiar with each essay. No admissions officer would ever admit a plagiarist.

A counselor from a prestigious prep school sent us this anecdote regarding our college *Essays That Worked* book:

When I was Associate Dean of Admissions at Georgetown in the (late '80s), we were asked to select memorable essays from among the applications of students who were being admitted. Two enterprising Yale graduates had requested samples of "essays that worked" to publish in a guidebook aimed at a high school audience. Because of our involvement in the project, we received several complimentary copies of the volume, which I read out of curiosity.

This background knowledge proved useful during my tenure on the George Washington University admissions staff in a subsequent year. Imagine my surprise when I reviewed an application, only to recognize one of the examples from Essays That Worked. *Although the student had elaborated on the original theme, the initial paragraph was word for word part of an essay that appeared in the book.*

The student who plagiarized was unequivocally denied, even though he would normally have been a good candidate. Instead of increasing his chances of admission, he instantly destroyed the value of all his academic achievements over three and a half years. I shared with his college coun-

selor the reason for our decision, knowing that the message would be re-layed to the student. What a shame! He didn't trust his own ability to be impressive enough.

The following pages demonstrate the creative potential of the law school application essay. We hope these essays will inspire you when you begin to write, and we hope they will give you the confidence to write a bold, personal piece that is truly your own and that will help an admissions officer see why you are special. Enjoy the essays, study them, and let them be a catalyst for your own creativity.

PYRO-IMAGERY OVERLOAD

A law school admissions officer noted that he could expect one metaphor in almost every essay. Before you decide to carry a torch for the same image, allow this flash to scald your mind: fire imagery is trite. Take our advice and don't get burned. No matter how incendiary your essay may be, extinguish the pyrotechnics. The lines below were taken from actual essays:

"My involvement with music sparked a passion . . ."
"My mind blazed with the possibilities . . ."
"My interest in law was kindled at an early age . . ."
"My passion was ignited from the day . . ."
"The memory of that injustice burnt within me . . ."

To Have What It Takes:
ESSAYS ABOUT CHARACTER

Law school—and the legal profession in general—is demanding. No admissions officer wants to admit students who are simply enamored of a career in law from watching the current hot lawyer show on TV. Law school means spending hours and hours, night after night, reading obscure cases written more dryly than your tenth-grade algebra text. It is not glamorous. It is rarely fun. Law school requires hard work, self-discipline, and a high tolerance for tedium and exhaustion.

If you have endured before, and done so with humor and good nature, by all means tell your story. Don't be a martyr, though. Whining complaints about all your hardships are tiresome. The reader will just think: If it was so bad, why didn't he do something else? Miserable students—even smart, hardworking, miserable students—can make everyone else miserable, too. No professor wants a classroom full of bright but depressed legal scholars.

High spirits, on the other hand, are infectious. In Thomas Kelly's essay, the playful tone makes you think he really enjoys living in the squalor of the West African bush. Since he can laugh about his fly-infested food and the battle to acquire it, a long night of study or a stressful trial should be a cakewalk to him.

The writer of the next essay does a good job of turning the problems she faced (some of which appeared on her transcript) into a story of personal victory. By itself, a low grade in sophomore French might have hurt her application. But with this essay, she was able to convince the admissions officers to overlook that lapse.

The third essay offers an authentic voice and an effective presentation of the applicant's skills and motivations. However, it's probably too long, and the recitation of GPAs is redundant.

The last essay presents the character of a young Southern woman as she developed her own goals in the shadow of a strong and successful mother. By describing moments of her life in a well-written, exciting style, she reveals traits that made her a successful student at one of the top law schools in the country.

THOMAS A. KELLY, III

For two years I have been a Peace Corps volunteer in the Republic of Niger in West Africa. I live in a grass hut in a tiny village called Fandou-Berri, sixty-five kilometers from the nearest city. I subsist primarily on a diet of rice, millet paste and leaf sauce. Once a week I travel twenty kilometers to the village of Hamdallaye where I can buy goat meat. Each time I walk away from the Hamdallaye market, having bargained for a fair chunk of meat, I think of Mrs. H., an attorney at Paul, Hastings, Janofsky and Walker in Washington, D.C. She was known in the office as the Velvet Steamroller. It was said that she could bargain the shirt off of your back and make you believe that you had gotten the better of the deal. When I was a paralegal, I admired her technique. Now I wish she could see me deal with the butchers in Hamdallaye.

Because there are no scales in the West African bush, meat is sold by the pile. Normally, an amount of money is stated in advance, then the size of the pile is haggled over. When buying meat in Hamdallaye the size of the pile depends on a confluence of factors. Is the butcher working alone, or does he have to demonstrate his business acumen to his fellow butchers by slighting the foreigner? Is he in a good or even charitable mood? This will determine whether he will follow the practice of throwing one last large chunk on the pile after the bargain has been struck—the butcher's version of the baker's dozen. I have learned to judge the butcher's expressions as I approach the meat section of the market, then isolate a sympathetic looking one.

Is the buyer in the mood to haggle? This can work two ways. Some days the best strategy is to stare expressionlessly at the pile as it mounts, guilting the butcher into being fair. Other days, particularly if there is a crowd for the butcher to play to, one must haggle aggressively for the entire second half of the pile. If the buyer's approach does not correspond to the butcher's mood and to the prevailing conditions, he is certain to come away the loser.

The object itself often looks decidedly not worth the argument. The various body parts, including gaping eyeballs and oozing entrails lie on the table intermixed with the choice cuts of meat. There is no Styrofoam to mask the reality of what happened to that goat just minutes before. So many flies swarm on the meat that the haggling must be done in a raised voice so that both parties can hear over the buzzing.

The butcher closes the deal by reaching for his equivalent of wax paper—a U.S.A.I.D. cement sack. He tears off a piece, smacks it, which sends a cloud of cement dust into the air, then wraps up the portion of goat meat for transport. The transaction is complete.

If there is, in the curriculum of the law school I attend, a course in bargaining, perhaps Mrs. H. and I can teach it together.

NAME WITHHELD

When I was ten years old, I had a feisty pony named Merrylegs. Every once in a while, as I teetered on her narrow backbone, she would get this wild look in her eye just before bolting off down the road. All I could do was hang on and pray that I wouldn't fall off and die. I managed to hold my ground (although sometimes I ended up there) for about five years, and then my legs sprouted down so that when I sat atop Merrylegs, if I rocked from side to side, I could feel the precious earth beneath my feet.

As a teenager, my legs were long and skinny—the perfect legs for a cross-country runner. All through high school I performed on the track and cross-country teams, running the two mile race with my dad on the sidelines keeping my splits on his Timex wristwatch. I was no champion runner. I don't remember ever breaking the tape to the wild applause of the fans. But I remember making it across the finish line every time—sometimes grimacing, sometimes smiling— never giving up.

College was another test of perseverance. As I watched my parents drive away in their stationwagon, the dust from Minnesota thick on the back window, I started to cry. I didn't know a soul on this sprawling Big Ten campus. And what did I know about Iowa, except that between each endless cornfield there was a pig farm.

Desperate for company, I went to church with a girl from my dorm.

When the kneeling bench was pulled out, I thought it was a footstool. I knew the Presbyterians didn't allow such comfort during church services, but these Episcopalians were all right. A perplexed glance from my dormmate was all I needed to quickly slide my feet to the floor. I spent prayer time ruminating about the congregation—they didn't all look like pig farmers to me. Maybe there was more to Iowa than I thought. There definitely was more to religion than I thought.

By second semester, sophomore year, I was waiting for my second wind. I was losing ground on my studies and losing sight of French altogether. Balancing academics and a social life was like teetering on a narrow backbone, and one night, determined to bail out of both, I hiked to the Greyhound Bus station.

I didn't board the bus, and graduated two years later. I knew that whatever challenges I had to face—grueling workouts, suicidal horseback rides, college—I could face them and I could learn from them. Even if I wasn't the top horsewoman or runner or English major, I was someone who would hang in there and see something through to the end. My most significant accomplishment has been to persevere.

NAME WITHHELD

Iam an extremely goal-oriented individual. Self-motivation has been an important impetus in my life. For example, as a high school senior, I set one financial goal for the next four years. I would pay all collegiate expenses without parental or governmental aid. Perhaps this was a bit zealous for an 18-year-old with only a token summer job. I decided that attending a regional campus for two years while working 15 to 35 hours per week would best help me recognize my goal. Frugality prevailed during this time. Now, as a college senior, I realize my goal may have been somewhat unrealistic, but I have paid for 80 percent of those expenses.

Second, I am a very organized person. During my freshman year of college, I implemented a system of budgeting my time. Each night, I began to allot the following day's time in half-hour increments. It is a practice I still maintain.

Third, I am a leader. Two roles I have played are important in this assessment. At age 19, I was selected to be foreman of a jury trying a criminal case in my hometown. I was by far the youngest of the jurors and was actively involved in every part of the deliberation, seeking out each juror's opinion on points made in discussion.

Lastly, being very personable, I feel, is one of my stronger attributes. My work experience provides the one best example of this. As a sales representative for a construction corporation the previous two summers in my hometown, I was responsible for meeting with five to eight customers per day in a dyad setting. Because in our market there existed no differential advantages between competitors, my job entailed getting the customer to believe in me so he would then believe in the company I represented. I had the highest sales-close percentage in the firm.

Several activities fill my free time. As a member of Beta Alpha Psi, the national honorary accounting society, I am currently involved with the Alumni Committee. We are working on a project to keep alumni informed of chapter events and, hopefully, we will deliver a newsletter to them in mid-December.

Sports have always provided me with great enjoyment. It was because of my love of children and basketball that I spent two years as head coach of a fourth-grade YMCA basketball team. It was one of the most fulfilling activities of my life.

Culturally, I am also intent upon expanding myself. I am captivated by the study of history, especially European political history as it pertains to the two world wars. I also have a keen interest in politics and, time permitting, will work in the upcoming election.

My greatest academic achievement, though, is that I have received a very intensive education in accounting along with a very broad diversion into many other academic fields. This education has rounded my individual being and, consequently, I am not just a business major.

My aspirations are to practice law in a business environment. I am enthralled by how law applies to business and the effects of the business community upon the formation of the law.

I will be successful in law school because my undergraduate work has prepared me. As I understand, four skills are necessary for an undergraduate to develop if he desires to do well in law.

First, developed communication skills are imperative. To accomplish this objective, I planned a curriculum that emphasized essay exams, term papers, classroom participation, and oral presentations. Fifteen hours of history, nine of political science, six of English, and three each of communication, philosophy, sociology, and psychology have I taken. My cumulative G.P.A. in the above 42 hours of coursework is 3.86.

Second, the above courses were also beneficial to me not in how they were taught but in what they taught. An understanding of society and its problems is an important asset for a prospective law student. The above courses are one avenue to a greater understanding of society and the role of law within society.

Third, many legal questions focus upon a business consideration. Thus, the prepared law student has an understanding of the business community and the implications of the law upon it. My coursework in finance, economics, marketing, operations, and accounting (my major) has provided me this knowledge. My cumulative G.P.A. in accounting is 3.66.

Lastly, logical thought processes are an important instrument for the undergraduate to possess. I have developed my analytical tools in nine hours of mathematics, six hours of science, and three hours of philosophy. My cumulative G.P.A. in the above courses is 3.5.

In conclusion, I must comment upon the wide disparity in my two LSAT sittings. During the month preceding the first sitting, I was experiencing some personal problems. I had not resolved them by test date and I feel they impacted negatively upon my performance. I resolved them shortly afterwards. For this reason, I feel my second score is more indicative of my abilities and I would ask you give that score greater weight when evaluating my potential.

ERIN SPIOTTA

When I was a baby, Mother woke me up each morning, strapped me to her back, and carried me to the courthouse downtown where we worked (snoozed and slobbered) diligently all day long in order to buy Gerber's and purchase Dad's medical degree. I grew up, tied to this intelligent and intense, obstinate and obsessed, strong and self-sufficient, steeped in the traditions of the deep South woman. I was reared wearing white gloves and reciting Rilke.

When I turned three, Mother taught me to address adults as "ma'am" and "sir" and how to count to ten in Spanish and in French.

When I turned ten, she showed me how to set a formal dinner table properly and told me I could go to an Ivy League school when I grew up.

When I turned fifteen, she instructed me on the importance of snaring a husband named Vanderbilt or Kennedy, and she made me promise never to forsake my goals or abandon my aspirations in order to be with a man.

As I approached eighteen, I began to kick and squirm, struggling to escape the confines of the backpack. I chose to go to Duke, "that cold, expensive school in the North."

As I launched my college career, I sought to define myself, to make my own decisions, to explore different people and to experience foreign ideas. I had the gall to date an improvident boy whose father had declared bankruptcy and the audacity to pledge a sorority other than Tri-Delta. What I called divergent value systems, Mother called spite; to what I considered to be independence, she gave the name BETRAYAL. Soon the buckles and straps which had held us intact dissolved entirely, and threats to be expelled from THE WILL were legitimated and surmounted only by the roaring silences which ensued.

I went to France my junior year. Somehow the strength and stature of Paris rendered me passive, awestruck. Rather than try to buck the flow of life and manipulate the course of events, I let the city speak to me. For the first time in my life, I, solitary, sat down to watch, to listen. Paris taught me not only about Picasso, surrealism, and good red wine, but also about family, about future. I realized that I admired and appreciated my mother and that perhaps it was possible for me to follow the parental prescription and go directly to law school without sacrificing the identity I had worked so hard to create.

When my family came to visit me, I got to be the master, the tour guide, the provider. I showed them my city, my methods of survival, introduced them to my successes and my failures. As Mother was boarding the plane back to Memphis, she turned to me and said, "Your grandmother called me the other day to wish me a Happy Birthday. For the first time in forty-four years she told me that she loved me and that she was proud of me. I want you to know before you turn forty-four that I love you, and I am proud of you."

The fighting is over for now; we gave up or grew up. We are trying to exist in tandem.

I returned to the States this year inspired and empowered, ready to engage and invest once again. I know now that my desires can concur with the wishes of my mother without being dictated or dominated by them. I can get a law degree that will not float in the shadow of hers and continue doing what I have always done—cheer for the underdog. From rescuing sand fleas stranded on the beach, to insisting that my best friend in the seventh grade, caught in the crossfire of a custody battle, live with me, to defending gays in my hometown, to standing up to my college roommate's abusive boyfriend, to expressing outrage at the guardian ad litem reports filed by my mother, I have always been an activist. I love to fight for the powerless, for those who choose the paths of most resistance.

I also love implicit moral rules. I remember once in high school after losing to a particularly inhumane soccer team, I was quoted in the newspaper as exclaiming in defense of my own team, "We prefer to play ethical soccer." Similarly, I would like to play ethical law, to have a role in cracking the media-thirsty and money-hungry lawyer stereotype. I like to play rough, to dance on the edge, but I do not lose quietly to cheaters. I would like to have the freedom to be an activist, a defender, of something other than my decision to attend law school!

I am intelligent and intense, obstinate and obsessed, strong and self-sufficient. I want the power to reach out and help change the lives of others and to expose truths rather than employ tricks. Why do I want to go to law school?

Not because my mother told me to.

Be True to Your School:
ESSAYS ABOUT WHY YOU AND
THE SCHOOL ARE WELL MATCHED

———————

All law schools are not alike. While admissions officers can quickly spot "sucking up," showing some knowledge of the school to which you are applying is a smart move. Law school readers, maybe better than any others, can recognize a canned, generic essay that you're sending to several schools. Law school is serious business; admissions offices want evidence that you understand the gravity of the coursework and that you've made an effort to treat your application to their school seriously.

Any indication that you have carefully considered the schools you want to attend can make you seem more mature and respectful. You want to persuade the admissions officer that you're a good fit with the school, but don't spoil your observations with effusive language and gratuitous praise.

"We get a lot of applicants trying to flatter us by writing something like, 'Your school has an internationally renowned reputation,' " one admissions officer said. "And you just know they wrote the same thing to twelve other schools."

Even if you honestly believe that a school has "an exciting and diverse student body, brilliant professors, and an excellent program of study," telling them this says nothing about you.

Every law school has some fine aspects, and a candidate who has researched the school can speak to them. Doing so could convince the admissions officer to let you in—or reject you. If you cannot substantiate your argument that you "fit" the school well, the admissions officer will see it as merely contrived—and, perhaps, you as merely desperate.

Yale Law School is known for its politically active, often left-wing students and faculty, and an essay about your compassion for the oppressed might be received well there. But if your history of activism consists solely of being treasurer for your high school's Young Republicans club, you're not going to need directions to New Haven.

The law schools at the University of Chicago and the University of Michigan are considered rather traditional, where your hard work may count for more than your politics. But telling the admissions committee in Ann Arbor that you are "inspired by the demanding workload at Michigan" will fall flat if your college grades are mediocre.

So consider a wide range of law schools, and if you find a terrific match for your interests, personality, and background, by all means exploit it. But don't try to stroke the admissions officers' egos or think you can take advantage of their naïveté. They've seen it all before, many times.

JEAN SKELTON FRASER

My grandfather, dean of the Minnesota Law School and alumnus of Harvard Law, had one thing to say about Yale Law School. "If you want to learn sociology," he said, "go to Yale. If you want to learn law, go somewhere else."

Though my grandfather may turn over in his grave, Yale is my first choice. As my parents have shown, an understanding of our legal system is of great value in effecting social change. I believe that my father's legal training has made him a more responsible and effective congressman and mayor. For example, he vetoed an anti-pornography ordinance—whose goals he agreed with—because it infringed upon the right to free speech. My mother, who has worked in and out of government, also stresses the importance of change within the context of existing institutions. Having been caught in Uganda during a coup, she is only too aware of the fragility of our defenses against rule by violence.

Only fair law justly applied keeps us from anarchy. Law is the expression of a complex interaction between our cultural values and the structure of our society. Because I want to change the attitudes and the structure, I need to understand our legal system, not just the law codes. What fascinates me is the process as well as the end product. At Yale I want to learn how our laws have been developed and applied in the past to be more effective at changing them in the future.

DANIEL KIEL

"What do you call a bunch of lawyers at the bottom of the ocean?"

"A good start."

It always seems to be the same punch line—the world does not need even one more lawyer. Swayed in my youth by these profound social commentaries (jokes), I concluded that I would not be a lawyer. I wanted to become a politician, instead, as if popular opinion were any gentler toward that profession. With this attitude and these plans, I applied for my internship at a congressman's home office—an internship that convinced me that even if the world did not need another lawyer, the study of law was the best future for me.

I arrived my first day on the job, my mind filled with images of witnessing politics from within and meeting people of great importance. What I failed to realize was that working for a congressman's Washington office and working for a congressman's district office involve very different tasks. While D.C. staffers research policy, work with legislation, and even mingle with public figures in the halls of the Capitol, the duties in the home office relate almost exclusively to assisting the district's constituents.

My first duties included acting as an apprentice to a congressional caseworker who was responsible for solving problems constituents encountered with federal agencies. I had the opportunity of working directly with people and after only a few weeks, I was given the responsibility of handling casework of my own. As I worked, I noticed a great deal of similarity between the jobs of a caseworker and a lawyer. Both have the responsibility of acting as advocates to a constituent in front of an institution. Both must fully understand a client's situation and translate it—to either a federal agency or a court. Both must present and argue their case to receive a favorable decision.

While I continued to enjoy working for the government, the passion I gained for assisting constituents helped focus my goals. I recognized that the aspect of politics that had drawn me was the prospect of helping people and I realized that in order to continue helping people, the study of law was the best future for me.

One case, in particular, convinced me that my goals and talents were best suited by a future in law. A constituent called, in tears at the way the Social Security Administration had treated her. This constituent's husband had recently passed away and the SSA was questioning her eligibility for benefits. Aside from the sympathy I felt for her being forced to fight over money under such circumstances, I thought she had a legitimate argument to receive the money. I requested the case and got to work.

My first step was to get a better grasp on what the Social Security code said about such cases and to write a letter explaining why the constituent was entitled to the benefits. My background as a history major came to benefit me, as I had to research and argue my point to convince the reader. I finished the letter, got the Congressman's approval, and sent it on to Social Security, confident that they would issue a favorable decision.

The response I received was disappointing. My case had not been clear enough and Social Security upheld the rejection. However, their denial seemed to overlook the circumstances of the husband's death—circumstances that I believed made her eligible for benefits according to the Social Security code. I sent a follow-up response clarifying my letter and waited again, eager to know if my argument had succeeded. The response came after several weeks and as I read the letter a smile crept over my face. The SSA reversed their decision and ruled in the constituent's favor. I called her to relay the good news and she joyfully and repeatedly thanked me.

This was just one of many cases I have had the opportunity to work on. Each case comes from a different constituent with a unique problem, so it is imperative that the caseworker be able to deal with many different situations. My experiences abroad, living for over a month in several foreign countries, have enabled me to adapt to unfamiliar situations and solve problems within them. This versatility proved useful as I was given more responsibility at the office and the nature of my cases increased in scope and intricacy.

Studying law in Washington at Georgetown fits both the initial goals I had when coming to work at the Congressman's office as well as the passion I gained there for representing constituents. My interest in government and politics has not waned, as I have remained politically active, specifically with my involvement helping to register over 8,000 students with Texas Youth Vote. However, my strengths in research and formulating arguments, as well as my resourcefulness and persistence, have convinced me that the study of law is where my future lies, no matter whether the world needs another lawyer or not.

Turning Points:
ESSAYS ABOUT IMPORTANT CHANGES

ow do you use your experiences to change and grow? The "turning point" essay can show how thoughtful, sensitive, and responsive you are, and writing it might give you even more insight.

One incident rarely changes a person's life. Trying to persuade the reader that a single event suddenly revolutionized your perspective on Life, the Universe, and Everything is likely to sound (and be) contrived rather than profound. Nevertheless, discussing a specific experience can be a great way to express a change or an idea that has developed over time.

The essay by James Silk is especially powerful. His final line—added, it seems, almost casually—will jolt the complacent reader. Even if you disagree with him, his essay shows an impressive understanding of issues, emotions, and the perspective on both sides.

Steve Peikin prods the admissions officer with a concluding waiver. Who knows what will happen to Peikin's fragile liberalism without the firm guidance of his professors?

Marian Macpherson uses a personal experience to resolve a larger question. With her exposure to Wood's Lab, she realizes that science and art can be compatible rather than antithetical.

Joshua Karsh sprinkles wit throughout his look at another age-old conflict. The twist comes at the end when he surprises the reader expecting yet another religious rebirth.

Finally, Jonas Blank writes with clarity, candor, and no sentimentality about his work experience in the office of a criminal attorney. To his surprise, he is forced to see the human side of a vicious killer and find the reasons to defend him. There is a maturity in Blank's style that made him an excellent choice for Harvard Law.

The "turning point" essay demonstrates that you can be flexible and that you are strong enough to reveal past ignorance—both admirable traits in a would-be lawyer.

JAMES J. SILK

My students waited for me in our cold, damp classroom. I counted on their unyielding eagerness, wit, and warmth and a bit of topicality to dispel the gloom of the Shanghai winter morning. An article in *China Daily* about the execution of a provincial party official for embezzling public money would stimulate a lively discussion. The article drew no response, but my questions about the death penalty elicited a unanimous defense of capital punishment. I clung to undogmatic questioning until my disappointment in the certainty with which even gentle Xiao Chen pronounced judgment outweighed class plans and my commitment to neutrality.

Their arguments never strayed far from the primacy of society over the individual. I recalled American generals observing that life in Asia was simply less dear. My rejection of that cliche undiminished, I was equally unwilling to accommodate the students' views through some more generous exercise of cultural relativism. Despite my appreciation of the cultural, historical and personal sources of their position, I could not leave it unchallenged.

If I referred to the irreversible consequences of a mistake, they assured me that the authorities arrested no one until thorough investigation established certain guilt. My assumption of innocence until proven guilty was not so obvious to them. If I said there was no evidence that capital punishment was an effective deterrent, they said it would deter the kinds of crimes against society that China needed to control. Surely, I said, death is cruel and unusual punishment, grotesquely in excess of the seriousness of such crimes. They found that an arbitrary classification; prison was also cruel and unusual. Furthermore, some crimes so damaged and endangered their fragile, new society that the most extreme punishment was necessary.

I mustered all my eloquence to argue that a state which ratifies death as legal punishment ultimately legitimizes violence and contributes to the very disorder it aims to deter. They responded that not to execute serious offenders was to legitimize the offenses and show the weakness of the state's will.

As class ended, one student dismissed my view as romantically moral, saying, "That's the difference between our cultures. Americans believe there is a right. We believe that what is necessary is right." In frustration at their stale utilitarianism, I resorted to an untestable and petulant last word: "As China develops, your attitude will change." Six months later, I came home to an increasing number of executions in the United States and arguments for them that were merely vengeful.

STEVEN R. PEIKIN

"How Can You Defend Those People?"

It is appropriate that James Kunen used this question to title his book about his experiences as an attorney for the Public Defender Service. During my summer as a Yale-P.D.S. Fellow, many people posed the same question to me, and I found myself searching for the answer as well.

I began work at the Public Defender Service feeling uncertain and apprehensive. As an investigator and case assistant for an attorney in the trial division, I was to direct my energies toward the defense of clients charged with serious and violent felony crimes. Our clients might be ex-convicts or drug abusers. On "the other side" stood the U.S. Attorney whose clients were justice, order, and the protection of society. I was not confident that I was on the side of right.

As the summer progressed, however, I witnessed the steady decrease of my uncertainty. My change in attitude reveals some important lessons learned. One of these lessons is that most people, as I did, foster a stereotypical image of "those people." The clients with whom I worked were not all ex-convicts or drug addicts. Nor, as many misconceive, were all of "those people" guilty of the crimes of which they were accused. Certainly many of our clients were guilty, but their guilt in no way precluded their right to the best possible representation. The only commonality which I could observe in our clients was an inability to pay for their own defense.

Anyone working in criminal justice must observe that the system is inherently weighted against poor people. If lawyers are valued by how much money they receive for their services, then poor people are most likely to receive the lowest quality legal representation. The apprehensions that I had about defending "those people" quickly fell before the realization that their poverty causes them to be treated as inferiors before the law. Working to help the small actor assert his or her equality before a large and powerful system seems like a worthwhile service.

My greatest uncertainty about working for P.D.S. stemmed from a preconception that defense attorneys work against the service of justice to let the guilty go unpunished. My conscience was eased by my observation that this is largely untrue. For the most part, the guilty are convicted when the evidence weighs against them. Further, our system of jurisprudence assures that the conviction of the innocent is extremely rare. But does this reality mean that justice prevails? In answering this question, James Kunen makes a very astute, if sobering, observation. He says that by the time a criminal case gets to court, almost all of the injustice has already occurred. "The victim has already been victimized; the defendant, more often than not, has been subjected to every kind of abuse, from inadequate prenatal care to exclusion from the work force." In such a framework, how can any court claim to administer ultimate justice?

During my time at P.D.S. I became extremely sympathetic to our clientele. The murder case that I worked on for most of the summer resulted in an acquittal, and I was extremely proud to have been part of the defense team. Nevertheless, there are aspects of criminal defense which still trouble me. Removed from the environment of P.D.S., many of my doubts about the role of defense attorney return. I anticipate that my legal education will enable me to explore this problem further and will allow me to consider it in a more enlightened perspective.

MARIAN MACPHERSON

What I Learned in Wood's Lab

At the University of the South there is a mysterious place called Wood's Lab where English majors do not go. Being a loyal and enthusiastic English major myself, I conscientiously shunned Wood's Lab until one day when, near the end of my fifth semester, I placed myself into a situation which would not only recquire me to enter that ominous building, but which would also teach me a valuable lesson about the relationship between the study of the arts, to which I was devoted, and the study of the sciences, from which I was trying to disassociate myself.

My adventure began when, while looking through the course list for my next semester's classes, I came upon the intriguing title "Cultural Anthropology of Appalachia and the South." Having grown up in the South, I am always interested in learning more about it, and this course, which proposed specifically to examine our culture, demanded my serious consideration. Although I saw that this course was scheduled to meet in Wood's Lab, I read the course description. When I discovered that William Faulkner's *The Sound and the Fury* was listed among the required texts, temptation and curiosity overcame my inhibitions. I registered to take Anthropology 309.

As the day of my first meeting approached, I began with horror to consider the ramifications of what I had done. I was going to have to orient myself to a whole new mode of thinking. Grammatical rules would not help me now. I was going to be on my own, surrounded by "scientific" people, in the dreaded Wood's Lab.

It was a great relief when I finally attended the first class and realized that all my fears had been groundless. The interior of Wood's Lab was as comfortable and as aesthetically pleasing as those of the buildings in which I took my English and French classes. The "scientific" people expressed themselves in comprehensible, even eloquent, terms, and the subject matter was just as interesting as I had hoped it would be. I learned much about the culture of which I am a part, but more importantly I learned that my literary background could complement my anthropological studies, just as my experience in Wood's Lab could enhance my appreciation of literature and the arts.

My anthropology class exposed me to a whole new realm of insights into *The Sound and the Fury*, and in writing my final paper on the development of Southern Literature as a distinct art form I found that there is an unbreakable bond between the study of art and that of science. The two are inextricably linked in a complex network of overlaps and divergences. To look at only one aspect of the network is to prevent yourself from seeing the whole truth of what you are studying.

For anyone to say honestly that he has a liberal arts education, he must be able to view the world from a liberal perspective. By venturing into Wood's Lab, I gained this perspective, and I will graduate from Sewanee in May, with the solid background I need to begin pursuit of a law degree.

JOSHUA KARSH

Towards the end of spring semester last year, posters appeared around campus announcing an "Ivy League Torah Study Program." The Lubavitcher Chasidim were offering select, Jewish college students an eight-week crash course in faith, *Chasidus*, and the world of our great-grandparents. My reading of Kierkegaard should no doubt have dissuaded me from such a program, but the chance to scout the faith-fed mind from the inside caught my fancy, and I signed on. Pitting three years of Ivy liberal arts education against eight weeks of Chasidic *yiddishe yeshiva* indoctrination, I reasoned that if the yeshiva were to win, my parents might at least file for malpractice against Yale in retaliation.

On the day of my campus interview, still elated by the tropes tossed out by my literature professor an hour before, I hurried into Career Services and headed toward the waiting area, where a lone, rabbinic-looking figure, barely visible behind his shaggy beard and underneath his black hat, stood mumbling Psalms to himself in a corner. "Text" was about to confront "Torah"; Yale to meet yeshiva. The Chasid in the corner looked up, and we greeted each other. That, however, was the last I said for several minutes, as he zealously prepared to set me straight. All the while waving his body back and forth, my Chasid began to explain that in spite of the "critical heresies" I had just heard propounded in the classroom, where the Torah was concerned the

Author would always defy the deconstruction of a Derrida. I listened patiently, nodded, suggested to this Chasid that the two of us had been nurtured on the same tastes of shmaltz and the same bedtime stories, and then offered that while I personally doubted whether the formula could be found which would square my view of things with his, I was still eager to see our shared palates and imaginations give it a try. He leaned back, whispered, "Have a little faith," and smiled.

Ten weeks later, I and sixteen other college *buchers* sat down oppo-site five rabbis, most of us to *"lerne"* the ways of their religious minds, most of them to rescue us from lapsed thought and act. Not surpris-ingly, certain snags soon appeared: "What about the archaeological evidence of this 7000-year-old . . . ?" *"Nu, vat by it?"* "Well, you claim the world is just 5700 years old . . ." *"Nu, nu?"*. . . . The difficulty was plain: for these spiritual virtuosos, the only logic linking one proposi-tion to the next was faith; but for me, the *logic* of faith was inscrutable. Borrowings from Tertullian's creed—*Credo, quia absurdum est* (these rabbis could only believe it *because* it was so absurd)—kept rushing through my mind, as I struggled to appreciate what it must be like to operate according to rabbinic logic, to find one's psyche tortured by crucifixion envy and one's intellect covenanted to a circumcision of reason. I did not think that I would ever understand.

The marvel, however, was that before long I did begin to under-stand. I even began to wish that I too might float—like the rabbis—on logical lacunae, might walk—like the rabbis—on water, so to speak. In the face of rabbinic virtuosity, all my old rules, all my old skepticisms, seemed to give way. Though theretofore "religiously un-musical" (Max Weber), I found myself suddenly yearning to chant and sing anyway, abruptly and unexpectedly persuaded that the songs the rabbis were teaching would somehow make harmonies of my con-fused and insistent dichotomies. Clashes such as those between fact and value, deed and creed, content and intent, art and act, and signifier and signified, all looked as if they might finally achieve resolution; for the rabbis' songs, like no others I had ever heard or learned, seemed to promise special secrets of sense, and of meaning. Daily, absurdity was becoming more manageable.

For weeks, then, I fought in earnest to learn to sing with the rabbis, to chant their tunes. But, foolishly, I mistook the proper tack. To sing, I figured, one surely had to sit down and practice the notes. So I sat down, and I practiced. But the notes finished, unavoidably, by blocking rather than clearing my way. Indeed, it was a long while until I realized what Kierkegaard should have made clear for me before, that one does not **learn**, or even *lerne*, to chant the tunes of the rabbis. Those tunes are **willed**; and he who would truly chant them must do so from the deeps of the soul, where no notes are ever found.

In the end, in the classrooms where I spend my time today, I am still learning from notes of sorts, and I am still battling the same dichotomies. But after my summer with the rabbis, I know now that neither notes nor dichotomies, nor the bulk of a college education, lend anything to the search for faith. Man may find many things by knowledge; but he finds faith only by unconditionally willing it. Unfortunately, willing like that amounts to volitional suicide; and I am not up to it. But oh, I wish that I were.

JONAS BLANK

That bone-weary misty October morning, in a little white brick building with red trim, I expected to do some filing, run some errands, and maybe finish some reading for class. I hoped for a slow, predictable day with few complications and plenty of time to focus on Duke work instead of Durham work, even though I was at my job. Instead, that morning found me face-to-face with hard, difficult facts and a complicated national moral quandary.

The building, in Durham's decayed historic heart, is home to the law offices of Loflin & Loflin, a two-person firm made up of Tom Loflin and his wife Ann. A few other attorneys rent the leftover space not overrun with old files and sports paraphernalia. Everyone in the building specializes in criminal law of some form or another, and they are a largely idealistic bunch—Alex, the police brutality expert, Marvin, the juvenile justice advocate, Karen, who was the city's first African-American female judge and Kevin, often swamped by pro bono work. I came to know Tom and Ann best, though, and their experiences and idiosyncrasies I understood most. They were also the only UNC-Chapel Hill graduates I've ever met who were rabid Duke basketball fans—they even had five season tickets.

This was not going to be an easy morning—in fact, I actually had to learn how to do something. Tom told me to take an affidavit from a woman named Betty and the little girl with her, Shawna. I had no more instructions than sit at the computer, listen to what they said and type it up coherently.

Betty and Shawna were the mother and daughter of a convicted murderer named Rick, who was making his final appeals before execution by the State of North Carolina. Rick and some friends entered a gay bar to find someone to rob. They met a man playing pool, and he took them back to his trailer home. While the man performed fellatio on his friend, Rick allegedly stabbed him in the back. He and his friends ransacked the trailer for some meager valuables and fled, leaving the man to die.

The affidavit was meant to be a character statement, to portray Rick as something beyond his deed. His mother's story was simple enough: Rick is a good boy who cares about every living creature and person. His life up until that day had consisted of many small, decent acts, from helping friends move in to working at a local animal hospital. Rick had love, Betty said—and he gave it. He loved little Shawna, sending her goofy cartoons of rabbits and tigers and rainbows from his prison cell. Sure, Betty said, Rick's told a lie or two and even gotten into a few scrapes, but his life—to be told through this series of petty anecdotes—was worth keeping.

Rick's childhood defies every notion of the American Dream. Betty—an ex-stripper battered by years of alcohol, cigarettes and bad relationships—was living hard in Fayetteville, NC when he was born. Rick's daddy rolled on without second thoughts, leaving the memory of beatings and pain in his wake. Betty's next men were no better—a string of swaggering alcoholics and renegade soldiers who left her and her young son with a bruised legacy of broken bones and thwarted hopes. By his twelfth birthday Rick had been sexually assaulted three times and diagnosed with a learning disability. Nobody was surprised when he had trouble in school. Perhaps nobody but his mother was surprised when he was arraigned for murder.

Betty's voice quavered and she wrung her hands, trying not to cry. I looked up from the keyboard and saw her eyes wincing with shame and it hurt me. It hurt because Shawna had to stand there through the embarrassing and awful story, and it hurt even more because this grim piece of history was being retold through my hands, and I only had the power to change the punctuation. Marching stutter-stepped across my screen was a man's life, reasons for him to live—and all that stood between him and his death were cats and cartoons.

Rick's story wasn't new—maybe not even remarkable—but hearing it in an office only a handful of miles from a campus teeming with the promise of having it easy reminded me how high the real world's stakes can be. Against the backdrop of my comfortable past, I could scarcely take stock of Rick's lost chances and colossal pain. I felt ashamed for Betty and her mistakes, ashamed for Rick and his stolen childhood, and ashamed for the State about to execute him. And I felt ashamed for Shawna, already living with the stigma of a daddy in jail, now with the possibility of not having a daddy at all. I had heard the sordid consequences of many people's mistakes in the past three hours, but none of them were hers.

I never got to take Shawna's affidavit—I had to leave the office at noon to drive to class. But she left me her own affidavit of sorts—a picture of a pony with the words "I love you, Jonas" scribbled in high-lighter pen across the top, just like her daddy liked to do for her. It's still on the wall in front of my desk, across the room from where more desperate mothers and daughters will sit.

Working for the Loflins did not necessarily convince me to become a criminal lawyer. But the experience of their office—the incredibly, awfully high risk that every case entailed—showed me what it means to give everything to what you believe in. They showed me what it means to be uncompromising in your beliefs and your defense of them. My life has been a pageant of realized opportunities. I have been fortunate to share the company of awesomely admirable people at Duke. But none of these overachievers, none of these aspiring scientists and writers and doctors, have a story quite like Rick's. And his reality, his story, deserves to be understood, too.

The Loflins' work wasn't merely a job for them, but a way of life. They do enjoy themselves, but they enjoy themselves because they love what they do and they do it as well as they can. That attitude took me places I never thought I would go as a student. From putting on concerts to working as a politics reporter in Washington to being an entertainment editor, I didn't always take it easy, but I always enjoyed what I was doing. I've stumbled over piles of sweaty, hallucinating children while covering a rave party and dodged paint bullets at an Army ROTC exercise the day after getting up at 5:30 A.M. to watch their morning workout. I have visited teens in prison and watched Duke work from the inside. My eyes have stayed open—both literally and figuratively—and I believe I am better for all I have seen.

I don't know if I will ever defend a client like Rick or meet another little girl just like Shawna. But I do know that whatever stories, whatever challenges I eventually come across, will get everything I have.

So You Want to Be a Lawyer:
ESSAYS ABOUT ENTERING
THE LEGAL PROFESSION

W hy should you get to avail yourself of the awesome resources of a great law school? Why should you get the thick
welcome packet next spring while 10,000 other applicants get the thin
"no thank you" letter?

One way to convince admissions officers that you deserve a space at
their school is to discuss why you want to be there in the first place.
People choose to become lawyers for many reasons. If your reason
is interesting and revealing of your character, it might make a great
essay.

The first four of these essays concern idealistic visions. The writers
claim that a law degree might empower them to give life to their
dreams of true justice, clean sports, social morality, or better education. But weary admissions officers can get cynical about proclama-
tions of social conscience. After all, does anyone champion injustice
or unfair sports? Be sure to support your assertions with concrete actions or anecdotes.

For example, in the first essay of this section, the student meticu-
lously documented his argument that the law is dynamic, evolving,
changing. He is clearly excited about the possibilities, and through his

essay, he provides powerful support for his inspiration to enter the legal profession.

The writers of the next essays are driven by their own restlessness—the search for meaning or stimulation. Such a motivation can be compelling, but take care not to grow too ponderous. Few admissions directors want to give a precious opening to someone who is exploring without purpose or direction. "If an applicant wants to search," one admissions officer said, "he should take a year off and travel or something. Law school is demanding, and if students are confused about why they're here, problems will arise. Only occasionally will intellectual curiosity itself be enough to warrant admission."

Whether you agree with that policy or not, you must be sensitive to a school's perspective. Never say you are "just looking." State your purpose in positive terms: "I want a broad legal training that will allow me to enter many new fields." If you're not sure why you want to go to law school, avoid the subject. Better yet—reconsider your entire application.

NAME WITHHELD

I can still hear it now, in a staccato rhythm: "The life of the law has not been logic; it has been experience." Professor Morton Horwitz would repeat this phrase again and again as he described the emergence of a critical movement in American law. This quote, taken from Oliver Wendell Holmes' *Common Law* (1881), exemplified a new approach to the law. Rather than mechanically applying established doctrines (logic), Holmes called for judges and lawyers to restructure the law to address problems in American society (experience). Holmes was responding to classical legal thinkers, such as Christopher Langdell, who had used older legal doctrines to oppose legislative reforms such as income tax, minimum wage, and maximum hours laws. Through Professor Horwitz's course, I discovered how Holmes' opinions—his skepticism of established legal doctrines and his belief in encouraging legislative innovation—helped spark a critical movement in the law.

In many ways, this exposure to Holmesian thought has influenced my own approach to intellectual problems. Whether doing research in the Roscoe Pound Papers or organizing programs at the University Lutheran Homeless Shelter, I have constructed solutions through a combination of skepticism and innovation. After these two challenging experiences, of academic research and social service, I now want to sharpen my analytical skills through formal training in the law.

And, as I think about my future career, I am intrigued by the prospect of employing this legal training as either a public interest lawyer, a civil rights lawyer, or a private lawyer.

I began applying Holmesian skepticism to the study of history while doing research for my junior tutorial paper on Roscoe Pound, an accomplished legal thinker and scholar. What do I mean by Holmesian skepticism? Well, in *Lochner v. New York* (1905), Holmes pronounced, "general propositions do not make concrete cases." In this phrase, he argued that the court could not take the principle of freedom of contract and apply it uniformly to all economic regulation; instead, the court needed to look at the specific facts of each case. Similarly, during my research, I remained skeptical of the dominant proposition on Roscoe Pound's later career, namely that he had become a reactionary. Using Pound's personal papers, I explored the specific facts of Pound's political and administrative affairs. Most legal historians had labeled Pound a conservative based on his public disagreement with Karl Llewellyn over the meaning of legal realism. But I looked beyond these sources and examined Pound's private letters to Sacco and Vanzetti's lawyers, his editorials in the *Boston Globe*, and his private memoranda to the governor. Based on this research, I argued that Pound was a legal pragmatist because he remained thoroughly committed to employing experimentalism towards reforming the criminal justice system. In the end, my paper was an attempt to present a new historical interpretation based on primary evidence. And, I believe that by studying law and making legal arguments, that I can apply these research skills to important legal disputes.

Like Pound, I am not simply interested in the law in theory, but also the law in action. Over the last year as director of the University Lutheran Shelter, I have tried to aspire to Holmes' desire for innovation by re-examining and enriching our programming. This past year, I have reemphasized the shelter's dual mission of (1) creating a safe, friendly community and (2) helping our clients find permanent housing. In an effort to improve our shelter community, I've set up an art program, established a bingo night, and arranged talks on politics and homeless legal rights. As for our shelter's second goal, I met with the directors of an employment services firm and the Greater Boston Housing Initiative, working with them to help our clients find employment and apartments. In addition to helping our clients obtain housing, it was important to me to make sure that after our clients left, they still had a network of friends and counselors. Because of this concern, I set up the Beyond Shelter program, a support group for our transitional guests headed up by a former guest.

From my academic and service experience, I have found interests in both employing logical arguments in academic debates and constructing innovative programs in social service. In "The Path of the Law" (1897), Oliver Wendell Holmes, Jr. talked about the importance and the limits of theoretical debate to the law. He said, "The training of lawyers is a training in logic. The process of analogy, discrimination, and deduction are those in which they are most at home." Like Holmes, I would like to apply this analytical method toward a thoughtful evaluation of problems in the law. I hope that by learning to construct and evaluate legal arguments that I can eventually represent those who are underrepresented, submit civil rights briefs for the government, or do transactional work in community development.

THOMAS WILLIAM ANDREWS

As I have grown older, the Constitution of the United States of America has become, for me, a sort of secular religious document. At the risk of sounding ridiculous, some people dream of joining the clergy, I dream of joining the bar. Some people feel drawn to Mecca or the Wailing Wall, I was drawn to visit Washington, D.C. and the glass-encased Constitution.

The Constitution is one of the things in this world that I choose to use to give definition to my life. I once tried to memorize it, but now I simply strive to understand it. I bought a facsimile of the Constitution in the gift shop of the building where George Washington was sworn in as our first President. It hangs on my wall as in other homes one might find a crucifix or menorah on the mantel.

I have heard people criticize the number of lawyers in the United States. The standard, simplistic comparison used is the ratio of lawyers to engineers in both America and Japan. While it is true that the United States has far more lawyers than any other society on the planet Earth, it seems also evident that we enjoy more justice than any other society on this planet.

We need people who know the law, and who push for justice, and who are uncompromising toward our freedom and rights. I feel there is always room for one more good lawyer. I want to be one of the people in our society trying to make the Constitution work, exercising our rights, and keeping freedom a strong and viable force.

MICHAEL HARRINGTON

"Al McGuire's Halftime Hoops" begins as the camera picks up the NBC Sports commentator walking across the beautiful North Carolina campus with alumni and sports attorney Michael K. Harrington.

McGuire: Walking around here, Mike, does it bring back memories?

Harrington: Yes, Al, and every memory is a positive one.

McGuire: What made you choose to be a sports lawyer?

Harrington: Many things, Al. I always participated in athletics myself and truly love the game of basketball. I guess I never really wanted to lose touch with sports. I also realized that there existed grave problems within the Sports Management arena. So I thought to myself that something had to be done to correct the wrongdoings of agents, and envisioned that I would be the man to achieve such a claim. Therefore, in many ways I rooted for the perpetuation of such corruption, solely because I wanted to provide the cure.

McGuire: You once said that your undergraduate schooling was chiefly responsible for your decision. How is that?

Harrington: Two reasons. First, I think that Williams College . . .

McGuire: The only school to ever deny John Wooden as a coach.

Harrington: The same. Incredible, right? Anyway, Williams allowed me to discover who I was. The smallness of the school breeds self-understanding, while also facilitating association with many others. Essentially, I learned a great deal about human beings and this enabled me to empathize with the plight of young athletes. I figured that if I was under pressure at 20, then so were they. Second, you have to remember that I was at Williams when sports agent controversies truly came out into the open. During my Junior year alone, an All-American in football and basketball respectively lost their final year of eligibility because they signed contracts too early.

McGuire: Did you find that North Carolina, specifically, helped you prepare for your future?

Harrington: Aside from my own knowledge and love of sports, North Carolina has meant everything. The legal training and education that I received from NC was outstanding, for it prepared me fully for my encounters in the "real world." Additionally, and very importantly, was the contact and exposure to the sports program at North Carolina, truly one of the most disciplined and demanding in the country. In fact, I benefitted immensely from my association with Coach Smith, who allowed me inside the basketball program, where I could further discover the mindset of the young athlete.

McGuire: You are currently doing very well. Are you satisfied?

Harrington: Yes, I am. You know, Al, the tendency in America is to measure success by how much money you make. To me, success means that I have helped a young and gifted, but vulnerable, athlete on the right path to a promising future. Realistically, sports law is a business for me, and I have to behave like a businessman sometimes. Fortunately, not that often. Thus far I have done very well without forgetting my purpose. It is very satisfying and comforting to know that I can be "successful" in this business without breaking the NCAA or professional rules. I am very proud of this, and elated to see more and more athletes adhering to the rules.

McGuire: Have you realized your dream?

Harrington: One of them, yes, I would like to think. If I have made athletes more aware of the consequences of signing early or accepting money, and been responsible for any one athlete to follow the rules, then I think my dream is realized.

McGuire: What's your other dream?

Harrington: To take your job away from you! (Laughter)

McGuire: Thanks a lot for your time and good luck in your future.

Harrington: Thank you, Al. GO HEELS!!

NAME WITHHELD

Currently, I hold a bachelor's degree in history and philosophy, and a master's degree in American Studies, from Purdue University, and I am a doctoral candidate in Educational Foundations, Policy and Administration at the University of Michigan. My primary interest in law arose from my studies of the organization and operation of American schools. Legal questions lie at the heart of nearly all controversies in public and private education; legal remedies, therefore, play a significant role in the resolution of these controversies. Also, many different forms of legal controversies are involved in education; there are contractual issues, other labor-management issues, and constitutional issues raised there on a regular basis. I wish to pursue a law degree for the practical purpose of helping to resolve these disputes and hopefully to contribute to the ongoing improvement of American education, and education in Indiana in particular.

Since the publication of several national reports critical of American education, state and local leaders have been re-examining their own educational programs and many have been making changes for the better. Laws governing education at the state level are a central element in maintaining a healthy system. And people who know the law and are committed to the area and to the health of the system are just as important. Having lived in central Indiana for eleven of the last thirteen years I have become settled here, have become committed to its development, and have come to know this area very well. In October I was elected to the Board of Directors by the membership of the West Side Food Cooperative and as the Board secretary by the members of the Board. From this position I have been able to begin to gain a greater understanding not only of business management but of the surrounding community as well.

My teaching, research, and writing experience have all helped prepare me for legal training. For two years as a graduate student at Purdue University I worked as a teaching assistant in the two-course sequence in American Constitutional History. I have also taught introduction to American History at Purdue University and Education in a Multi-Cultural Society at the University of Michigan, each of which necessarily dealt with legal affairs. I have gained considerable experience in legal research from graduate school coursework, as well as from research outside specific courses. This year, for instance, I assisted in the production of a Danforth Foundation conference paper on challenges to U.S. Supreme Court rulings on educational issues.

NAME WITHHELD

Like many, I suspect, who have been born into opportunity—into relative affluence and some intelligence—I have had difficulty eliminating the possible. This may not be a worthy lament, but it is a genuine one, one which has claimed much of the eighteen or so months following my graduation from college.

The typical college student comes upon graduation as upon a precipice, and many months of obsessive communal anticipation somehow fail to mitigate the abruptness of that moment in which he or she finally toes its edge. For the summa cum laude graduate of an elite school, this precipice is high indeed: so high, in fact, that he is told "the world is at his feet." At his back, thrusting him forward, is a life of high achievement on a carefully mapped, gently sloped course. Before him is, well, everything. A keen sense of incipient adventure might constitute an admirable response to such a predicament. Dizziness would not be inappropriate.

My own sense of vertigo upon leaving Dartmouth was steepened by conflicting forces within my personality. These cross-currents appear to me now as quite distinct, and their respective origins are easy to trace. From my mother I have inherited an impulse which one might generously deem "artistic." It prescribes a disengaged but highly sensitized observation of the world, a perception that is oblique and highly personal. It involves but it does not implicate. There is a certain uncluttered freshness to its vision.

From my father I have inherited a grasping analytical curiosity as to the "how" of things, an urge to explore and penetrate the workings, the machinations, of government and business and other sectors of our society. This current demands that one get in there and mix it up. It aspires to competence in the ways of the world, delighting, exulting even, in an involvement that is both intimate and intricate. It is the force which energizes the "problem solver."

These two impulses subscribe to different kinds of vision and strive for different kinds of understanding. If integrated, intuition tells me, they carry the promise of a rare and powerful synergy. Left in turmoil, I am equally sure, they can confuse, dispirit, and ultimately even paralyze.

You can probably envision me as I left school, bubbling like a cauldron. I was unwilling to emulate the precise and, as I saw it, mainly uninformed steps of my classmates. My ideas were broader. I had invested my high school earnings in the stock market at the beginning of this latest protracted bull market and so felt that, for a while at least, I could afford broad ideas. I thought in terms of "exposure," which, it turns out, I was to acquire through a series of false starts. A year's exposure to a foreign culture and language was cut off at six weeks thanks to newly stringent French labor laws and a companion's change of plans. Next I sought exposure to journalism and to New York City. I was exposed to (in?) New York for only three months, as my exploration of journalism there was limited to a basketful of "not hiring" notices (not to mention a daily scouring of *The New York Times*). At this point I was ready to come in from the cold for a time, which meant returning home and resuming my work as an editorial and research assistant on a projected law school textbook, just then consigned to a new round of revision. My efforts here focused on the metaphysical labyrinth of intellectual property law as applied to computer software and hardware. It was familiar and engaging work and lasted until the project was terminated.

Ultimately, "exposure" came to mean exposure to myself. The vehicle for this final definition was my decision to indulge a lifelong fantasy by devoting a year to writing fiction. Writing fiction consists largely of eliminating the possible, which makes it good practice for post-graduate living. The rest of such writing is, paradoxically, the preservation of the possible. As you might guess, I am most adept at this second task. I have been engaged in balancing those two objectives for several months under the cover of an eclectic range of occupations (ice cream man, waiter etc.). I am not quite sure what to make of the product of these efforts (an ambivalence which, I assure you, does not extend to waiting tables). But I have no doubt the experiment has been worthwhile. Its value inheres not so much in the daily exercise of writing itself, or even in the product of that exercise, but rather in the decision to step into the world calling oneself, sincerely, a "writer." The fallout from this commitment constitutes something like a visit to certain new age beauty parlors. One emerges, I imagine, with the wax removed from one's ears, the hair snipped away from one's eyes, and an entirely new layer of skin to meet the breeze.

In the end, however, more than anything else, writing means returning to oneself. It is thus among the loneliest and most self-indugent of occupations. And, at this point in life, there is a discomfitting pretentiousness to it, as well. One can wallow in one's own existence for only so long, and I'm beginning to recognize a need to get out of that mud.

Sometimes the dizziness of the recent graduate gives way slowly to the vaguest kind of disappointment, an amorphous burden attached somehow to the irrevocable linear momentum of living. He or she comes to realize, perhaps with undue emphasis, that each step taken is done so to the exclusion of all others. To walk through one doorway is to imagine hearing a thousand other doors slam shut. The only way to preserve pure possibility, that state of mind in which the talented and open-minded undergrad peruses his own potential, is to stand perfectly still, which, of course, gets you precisely nowhere. For one born at the altar of opportunity, this discovery that freedom does not feel like freedom can be as unsettling as betrayal.

I wish I could say I am applying to law school as part of some grand scheme to change the world, to leave it a little more just or even a little more efficient. But I am not sure such a thing is feasible, at least by design. Nothing is quite so neat for me. This is instead very much a personal decision, one inspired by my own needs, certain and uncertain. I have thought long and hard about how best to reconcile my disparate natures. And I am doing my best to eliminate the possible in favor of the actual.

CHARLES E. VALLES

S ocrates once said, "An unexamined life is not worth living." Well, here it goes.

For the first eighteen years of my life, my parents led the tedious task of convincing their only child that an uneducated individual was mercilessly destined to lead an unsuccessful life. In the Valles household, Education = Money = Success = Happiness. The beneficial qualities of an enlightened mind were secondary considerations, instead, primitive scare tactics were employed. How vividly the memories of youth endure . . .

. . . standing at my mother's side in line at the neighborhood Taco Bueno, and to suddenly hear that soft, protective, maternal voice approach my eager, impressionable young ears and whisper something like, "Charles, do you see that cook behind the counter, the one with the tattoo and the earring and no teeth?" Oh, so slowly I would raise up on my toes and peer, neck outstretched, until I managed to locate the unfortunate subject of the day's session of "LESSON IN LIFE, PART 783," and having done so, would turn back to my mother and, anticipating yet another horrifying story, would hesitantly respond "Yes, mommy?" Now my mother, never one to be accused of sanding down rough edges would say, "I'll bet you a dollar," one of her favorite expressions, "that he never finished school, has at least ten or twenty illegitimate children, is an habitual dope addict, doesn't have the slightest clue where his mother is, is probably wanted by every law enforcement agency in the western hemisphere," and for the grand finale, "and will be working at this SAME JOB FOR THE SAME PAY twenty years from now, that is if he doesn't murder everyone in the place one afternoon." Quizzically, I would again peer up and over the counter for another glance, quietly praying to the heavens that this would not be the fateful afternoon which would witness such misery, at least until my mother and I were safely distanced from this psychopathic haven.

For the first eighteen years of my life, I enjoyed the material benefits of a thriving Texas oil economy. Particularly throughout my high school years, a generous parental pocketbook, with the exception of working a few hours a week at my father's real estate office, replaced the vile necessity of sacking groceries at the neighborhood Safeway. However, growing up economically OVER-advantaged had serious unanticipated drawbacks. When I graduated from high school, I had simply had no desire to continue. I was bored with academics. My world became centered around athletic excellence and soccer expertise, and it was to this end that I dedicated my ambitions. From the time I was eleven years old I had planned to get my real estate license after high school and begin working for my father, an idea which my parents had gradually come to accept. Only when the world oil glut sent the Texas economy spinning did a college degree become a realistic probability. Not until one month before the first day of classes in the fall was I absolutely sure that I would be attending college. An advanced education had become a sudden, cruel necessity, not a welcomed endeavor.

It was no surprise, then, when I decided to enter S.M.U. What better place to spend four years than at a university since referred to by the *New York Times* as "Camp Wonderland," where the lobby of the new student union features marble tables and Persian rugs, and a shuttle service is operated, despite the size of the campus, to insure that our Reeboks don't wear out too quickly. I was prepared for a four- year vacation and I got stung, period.

For the lack of nothing better to do, I began to pursue a degree in business. Quite honestly, it was the most miserable experience of my life, an experience which was accurately reflected by my performance in the first three semesters. What material I did absorb was committed to short-term memory for test purposes, and soon thereafter forgotten. In the spring semester of my sophomore year, quite by luck, I registered in an American Government and Politics course. It was my saving grace. After three semesters of memorizing methods of calculating depreciation and interest rates, I was exposed to the opportunity of expanding intellectually, to analyze and criticize, not merely memorize. Faced with an opportunity for what I saw to be a refreshing change of pace, I began to wholeheartedly exploit the liberal education, and redirected my degree plan toward Political Science. Slowly, I was able to focus the ambitions and desires which had carried me across the soccer field for so many years into a desire to broaden my mind. The resulting change in academic performance was tremendous.

My last four semesters of studies have shown that I have an intellectual potential which has only begun to emerge. The liberal arts degree has fostered the growth of critical skills of evaluation as instruments of reasoning. Combined with a healthy exposure to both business and economics, and an active participation in extracurricular and cocurricular activities, the liberal arts curriculum has provided a course and means of self-discovery. Paradoxically, more education has left me less satisfied than did my high school experience. Learning has become an obsession. As a student at the Boston University School of Law, I will continue to pursue my current journey toward intellectual expansion and excellence.

NAME WITHHELD

My reason for wanting to study law are manifold, yet they all focus on the same end—a fuller realization of my utility as a person, mother, wife, worker and citizen. Since first encountering it many years ago, I am still struck by the wisdom in an aphorism of Benjamin Franklin, which I will paraphrase here—"the measure of a thing's worth is its utility."

As a person, I have been given, and have attempted to continue developing, a certain intelligence. I feel that it is my personal responsibility to extend this development and to now focus it on the study of law. After working for nearly five years in this field, I am more intrigued than ever with the law—what are its bases? its rules? its theory? its application? Working within the field has whetted my appetite to learn the hows and whys of law. I am increasingly frustrated with my daily work, which is tangential to the practice of the law; I am much more interested in reading and analyzing the arguments in a pleading than getting it neatly filed away. On a purely personal level, I will be a more satisfied and challenged person—a more *useful* one—if, after my formal study of the law, I can join what I learn with my life experience and intelligence to yield a more highly productive individual.

As a mother, I have provided the customary support, love and guidance to my children. I began and finished my undergraduate work during the years that my sons were quite young, and I believe that we have all benefited from the process. Although my parents are not college graduates, my sons regard a college education as a given. In our home, we customarily talk about ideas. The children have been nurtured on questioning, analyzing, critiquing and proposing alternative solutions. My study of law will not be isolated; the children will be included and they will grow in insight and aspiration as a result.

Having a husband who is an attorney has proved to be an invaluable source of information. Many of our conversations center around legal issues. I know that my study of the law will augment, refresh and clarify my husband's understanding of the subject, while his growing practical knowledge will certainly supplement my effectiveness. My law school experience will be a truly family affair.

As a member of society, a worker and a citizen, I feel that practicing as an attorney will more nearly fulfill my potential to contribute to my generation, my country and the future. I am sure that the study of law will sharpen and deepen my understanding and respect for the principles upon which our society is founded.

To sum up, I feel that my study of law has a unity of purpose. It will yield not only personal growth and self-realization, but will enhance the intellectual and social development of my sons, provide my husband a sounding board (and sometimes, a foil), and produce in us at least five more useful members of society, better citizens all. In years to come, I intend that this benefit have a wider application through service to the profession and the larger community.

NAME WITHHELD

The picture of Neil Armstrong first walking on the moon is still ingrained on my mind. It was seeing him on the moon that created my desire to leave the ground. As a child, I used to watch airplanes fly overhead, all the while dreaming that someday I too could leave the shackles of the ground. After years of dreaming, I can fly. I can leave the ground and fly into the blue infinity. The serenity of flying above the beautiful earth, above the rush of people, is quite relaxing. I knew as a child that I would love flying; I just did not know how much.

I dreamed other dreams as a child. I dreamed of becoming a policeman, a fireman, an astronaut, and an attorney. All but the latter dream have fallen from view. My interest in law and the legal profession has only increased since childhood. In college, I found my interests and abilities to be closely matched in law-related areas. I need to know that the work I am doing makes a difference. After spending two years in the business school, I found the emphasis on the bottom line to be less than fulfilling.

I also enjoy challenging myself. I like going beyond what I am currently capable of doing. One of my greatest challenges is helping people. In my fraternity, I have been fortunate enough to hold leadership positions from Parliamentarian to President. I find no greater joy than helping others achieve their goals. I use all of my abilities to their fullest when leading others. Being involved in extracurricular activities has improved my interpersonal and public speaking skills. It has also helped me to look more closely at all sides of an issue, to be more objective. I have learned through my leadership positions how to make difficult decisions. I have gained experience through extracurricular activities that hours in the library could never have taught. The challenge and experience gained from these activities has only encouraged me to continue my involvement in law school.

The summer jobs I have held have not only put money in my pocket, but they have also helped affirm my desire to attend law school. For three summers, I worked for an electronics supply company. The work involved numbers and limited human contact. It was not challenging. For one summer, I worked as an intern for a state games competition. The hours were long and the work difficult. It was all worth it, though, to see the happy faces of both children and adults at the opening ceremony and during the Olympic-style games. Working with people is much more challenging.

From flying to triathloning to practicing law, I need to know I am doing things I enjoy, that I am doing things that are challenging. I am ready to start a new education, one to which I have long been looking forward. I may not be able to walk on the moon, but I am able to contribute in my own way, by becoming an attorney.

In Honor of Thoreau:
CONTEMPLATIVE ESSAYS

The serious, philosophical "thought essay" is perhaps the most difficult essay to write. The best examples demonstrate an intellectually curious and disciplined mind, but even the best can be hard to read. Frequently, the essay loses its impact because students digress and let their logic get muddled by "ten-dollar words" and complicated strings of sentences.

Most students are too abstract when they discuss philosophical concepts in an application essay. When you write about an abstract idea, link it to something tangible with which the reader can identify. For example, you might use the death of a friend as a starting point for a discussion of religious philosophy. Remember, too, that admissions officers are pressed for time. If your essay doesn't grab them in the first few sentences, they won't keep reading. They don't have all day to kick back and contemplate your deep, brilliant insights.

Emily Nozick, for instance, sticks to eating habits and animals—things familiar to everyone—to illustrate how she has developed her worldview and reconciled emotion with intellect. Notice that she begins with a line calculated to perplex the reader without confusing him. After reading her first sentence, you're not sure what she's talking about, but you want to keep reading. She piques your interest, and reading her essay becomes a pleasure, not a chore.

What if Nozick had written a more typical, "safe" essay on the same topic? Her first line might read something like this: "Throughout the history of humanity, the intellect and the emotion, two characteristics that uniquely define the human in the animal world, have been locked in conflict."

Want to read more? Didn't think so.

Interestingly, when we requested essays from applicants, about a quarter were "thought essays," usually on some difficult legal issue, and almost all were tough to read. But when admissions officers sent us their favorites, only a few were on philosophical topics. After all, if you were forced to read 300 essays a day, would you rather read Immanuel Kant or Mark Twain?

We don't want to scare you, though. A "thought essay" might be perfect for you. The essays in this section are both interesting and effective—and they worked. Write clearly and make sure your ideas flow. Don't make assumptions about the reader's knowledge, and don't make mental leaps that leave the reader with brain cramps.

At the same time, you can't risk sounding pedantic or unsophisticated. Lecturing on the law before you have studied it is likely to bore and irritate admissions officers. No matter how great your legal contributions will be someday, it is far safer—and more revealing—to discuss your vision than your knowledge.

EMILY NOZICK

The material of my shoes has always been a point of discomfort for me, and the subject has arisen a remarkable number of times in conversation. It is not that my shoes are made of anything unusual—they are made of leather—but when I claim to be a vegetarian on moral grounds, one of the first attacks is always aimed at my feet.

I am never quite sure how to respond to this accusation of hypocrisy, and I have fallen back on the idea that I am "doing what I can," although I do not hold my head high when I give this retort. At the same time, however, I am somewhat taken aback by their response. It seems that, although I have never voiced it as anything other than a personal choice, people are automatically defensive around vegetarians and seek either to explain their own eating habits ("I only eat red meat twice a week") or to attack mine ("I've heard that plants scream when you cut them"). Why does vegetarianism elicit such a probing series of questions about exactly what you eat, what your grounds are, and how you justify other areas of your life? Does punching a hole in my behavior enable others to eat their hamburger in peace? Inconsistency in practice, it seems, is the downfall of any theory.

Nonetheless, the questioning has forced me to examine my views, and to reevaluate my original reasons for holding them. I first made up my mind to stop eating meat, chicken, and fish at our Thanksgiving table when I was three. No elaborately reasoned theory contributed to this decision; no pro-con arguments were weighed in my mind. I reacted from pure emotion. I had just seen a live turkey, who was looking perfectly content with his life, and here was an almost unrecognizable turkey, inert on the table. It just did not seem fair. But while my "this turkey wanted to live" statement adequately captured the line of reasoning of a three-year-old, I no longer feel comfortable maintaining a toddler's view of the world. At 20 years old, I feel pressured, both from others and from myself, to present a perfectly coherent picture of my sympathy for animals. Either the belief must encompass my practices of wearing leather and killing cockroaches in the bathroom, or my practices must change.

Unfortunately, a flawless system of action is not easy to obtain. Either the theory has gaping holes, or the practice is just too strenuous and demanding. But isn't remaining faithful to a spotted theory intellectually dishonest? How can inconsistency in action be explained?

With vegetarianism, I have to admit that in addition to the issue of inconvenience, my actions reveal the triumph of emotions over intellect. I do what I *feel* driven to do, and I ignore what I am ambivalent towards. I feel a "turn of the stomach" at the thought of eating meat, and not at the idea, or the action, of wearing leather. I certainly do not feel repulsion at killing a cockroach; in fact, I am disgusted by the idea of letting it roam free. All of my life I have acted on this one feeling of not wanting to eat animals, and I have not worried about the actions surrounding it. Perhaps it is artificial to now start molding some all-encompassing theory out of pure emotion. For even if I succeed in creating a view to fit my practices or vice versa, feelings of apathy or disgust have the first and final vote in this issue for me.

This is interesting, because in so many aspects of my life I hold up reason as supreme. I myself, like those who criticize me, have always had contempt for hypocrisy, or even an appeal to psychology over intellect. Such practices seemed weak. And here I am falling into the trap of irrationality of the very issue which, on the surface, stands on a pure intellectual decision. But to be honest, although it may be weak, I really think that emotion ultimately motivates my choice. After 17 years of being a vegetarian, and of thinking that it is "right," for whatever reasons, it is a part of me. I am comfortable with this belief, and no amount of prodding can shake me from the emotion. I guess that while intellect grows between the ages of 3 and 20, emotions stay pretty much the same.

ELIA FISHER

In his essay "Can Retributivists Support Legal Punishment?" in the *Monist*, George Schedler argues that a retributivist cannot consistently condemn telishment as unjust while supporting a system of legal punishment. Telishment, which is the inflicting of punishment on innocent people for an ulterior motive, has been objected to by retributivists in that doing so is inherently unjust. Schedler argues that since all systems of legal punishment will, on occasion, mistakenly punish innocent people, consistency demands of the retributivist that he reject all systems of legal punishment and not only telishment.

Schedler's argument contains two minor fallacies which I will discuss before elaborating upon the major flaw in his argument. His assumption that all systems of legal punishment must eventually punish people is not true. A system which admits only the most impartial of evidence and operates for only a finite period of time will not necessarily punish any innocent individual. This refutation, however, merely weakens Schedler's argument. For the great majority of systems, which are not set up in this manner, his argument would still be valid.

Schedler also incorrectly ignored the distinction between intention and knowledge of punishment of innocent people. It is true that many retributivists object to telishment simply because it results in the inflicting of punishment upon innocent parties. However, other retributivists, Kant among them, discuss the motivation behind the inflicting of telishment. Schedler's argument is valid only for the former group, since legal punishment is not implemented with the intention of punishing any innocent person.

Neither of these refutations has succeeded in rendering Schedler's argument entirely invalid. The more fundamental problem with Schedler's argument lies in his viewing legal punishment and telishment as systems rather than as particular instances. The retributivist's supporting a system that he knows will eventually punish an innocent person is entirely beside the point. The system is nothing more than the sum of many particular instances of punishment, and in each particular instance, the official believes that he is punishing a guilty party. On the other hand, every particular case of telishment is implemented with the knowledge that an innocent party will suffer. It is the particular case of telishment that the retributivist condemns, and the particular instance of legal punishment which he advocates.

It was not the purpose of this essay to deny the possibility of a retributivist coming to the decision that he cannot tolerate legal punishment. Rather I have demonstrated that Schedler's argument, as a proof that the retributivist cannot consistently support legal punishment while condemning telishment, fails.

NAME WITHHELD

The Benefits of Humanistic Approaches to the Study of the Law

Much criticism recently appeared in popular periodicals concerning the "criminal" way law is taught in schools. Oddly enough, this criticism makes me all the more attracted to a legal education. For at least one effect of this criticism is a more humanistic approach to the study of law. This change benefits not only legal studies, but the humanities, and possibly even modern culture itself.

Most forms of modern humanism assume a world that is inherently senseless. The humanist's task is not to find meaning in an external, objective reality but to impose meaning on what is otherwise chaos and inhuman homelessness *(unheimlichkeit)*. The problem with the humanist's program is that the humanist himself, as the acknowledged legislator of the world, has no authority. His values and meanings are his own creation and thus mere fictions; he cannot escape his assumption of an absurd world.

Humanistic approaches to the study of the law provide a means of grounding humanistic values. Legal institutions are at the center of American culture; they reflect and, to some extent, foster values. Because of this institutional anchor, humanistic legal studies give authority and credibility to humanistic values. These values become not mere fictions, but institutional realities.

The study of law thus enables humanists to reinstitute their meanings and values in a culture very badly in need of them. And in turn, humanistic approaches give legal studies a richer and more interesting context.

CRAIG COBEN

One often hears that fluency in foreign languages has many practical purposes and opens new career possibilities. Indeed, language proficiency is a useful skill in international trade, finance, law and diplomacy. For me, however, foreign tongues also represent the best of a liberal arts education: languages enhance my ability to understand what other people do, create and articulate. If one of the primary goals of a liberal arts education is to liberate students so that they may have choices in the shaping of their lives and in defining the needs of society as citizens, the study of foreign languages will contribute to this objective. Languages expand the freedom of a student, exposing him or her to different modes of thought and widening his or her horizon of civilization. Foreign languages have consequently always interested me, and I have devoted much time to learning them well. I speak Spanish and Italian very fluently and French reasonably well, and this year I am studying Swahili.

The shock of recognition in any intellectual field is intensely gratifying, and comprehending a text written in a foreign language produces an extraordinary feeling of accomplishment. Listening to the unmediated voices of Cervantes, Calvino, or Stendahl speaking from the fundaments of human experience, I experience pleasures of understanding for which there is no substitute elsewhere. Reading the actual accounts of the first Spanish *cronistas* (chroniclers) of the New

World and their attempts to come to grips with what to them was a completely alien culture, I sense a special immediacy to the Conquest of America. The original text stimulates my historical imagination about words and events that makes them much more interesting. When I grasp the wit of a pun or the subtle irony of a literary passage in a foreign language, I realize the inherent inadequacy of translation, no matter how skillfully the English version may have been rendered; I also experience the delightful feeling that I know the language not as just a series of symbols to be translated awkwardly into English, but as a living medium of communication endowed with its own ways of explaining the world. Furthermore, looking at a text in a language I do not know, I still try to decipher its meaning; the text seems almost a sacred arcanum whose holy mysteries are wrapped in words and symbols I cannot understand. I feel impelled to find my way into the obscure text. These struggles for understanding human expressions of many kinds and for making a foreign language less "foreign" leave an indelible mark on my sensibility.

The words of foreign languages reveal something about the psychology and culture of a people and thus provide me with a different perspective of life. My recent five-month odyssey through Southern Mexico and Guatemala underscored the importance of foreign language acquisition. A religious festival I witnessed last spring in the jungle village of Tenejapa, Mexico, would have seemed merely a quaint indigenous ceremony, if a gentleman there had not explained to me in Spanish the sacred meaning of the dances and apparel of the procession leaders. Tenejapa is an isolated hamlet attracting few Western travelers, and a good knowledge of Spanish (or the local Mayan dialect) furnishes the chance to unearth a few nuggets about the world-view of the Tenejapan Indians of Southern Mexico.

Unfortunately, Americans have the dubious but probably deserved reputation of generally refusing to learn foreign languages. This monolingualism often reflects an ignorance or even disdain of foreign cultures. In the increased interdependence of the modern world, this incapacity to understand people of other cultures is often embarrassing and sometimes dangerous to the national welfare. Such a peculiarly pre-Copernican focus—the ethnocentrist sees his or her own culture as the spiritual center around which the rest of the world revolves—spawns suspicion and mistrust between different ethnic groups and nationalities. I immerse myself in foreign languages, literatures and cultures to combat a crude world devoid of understanding. As a group Tour Director in Spain and France, I tried not only to find lost luggage at hectic airports, but also to convince my American clients that other people have very good reasons to be proud of their idioms, ethnic heritages, and distinct traditions. I hope that, when they think of Spain, some clients will remember not just such touristy goodies as Lladro porcelain and Majorica pearls, but also the architectural splendor of the Alhambra of Granada and the reasons for the triple character—*alcazaba* (fortress), *alcazar* (palace) and *medina* (city)—for this Moorish complex.

Foreign languages require much time and patience to learn, and speaking another tongue often produces feelings of uneasiness in the beginning. Nevertheless, the benefits of understanding other people and of communicating with them reward those efforts. Learning a foreign language expands one's vision prodigiously into a whole new realm of human understanding. Foreign language acquisition is necessary to be an educated, sentient person with empathy for foreign peoples and cultures and a capacity to experience the world through other eyes and other words. By helping me understand other people, languages help me understand myself and thus sustain my continuous endeavor to discover what is worth learning and doing.

JAMES TOURTELOTT

In answer to the instruction to "Write an essay on the subject of your choice, not to exceed 250 words"—

As a man who has earned his living by designing essay questions and reading semi-literate responses to them, I have some sympathy for the beleaguered members of admissions committees who have to slash their way through forests of dangling participles. As a man who spends more time providing writing samples than he expected to at his age, I have also become fascinated by the forms which requests for such samples take.

There are two fundamental varieties of such essay questions—the inordinately detailed and the deliberately vague. The one example of the inordinately detailed essay question with which every applicant to law school is acquainted is the LSAT writing sample, the setting forth of which is as jammed with unnecessary information as a political press conference. There is of course a reason, or at least an excuse, for this. The details are meant to furnish a basis for argument. Why one cannot trust a group of reasonably intelligent folks to dream up a line of argument I do not know, but perhaps there is wisdom in not encouraging people who plan to practice law to embroider on reality.

If the LSAT writing sample question is elaborate, the question I am answering is more streamlined. The advantage of this form is immediately evident: the English major can recycle his old Byron notes instead of trying to explain Marbury versus Madison; the poli. sci. student can expatiate on Gramm-Rudman instead of manufacturing acceptable reasons why he wants to study law—the prospect of a Mercedes not being the sort of thing one can mention in such circumstances. There are of course dangers for the respondent to such a question: the impassioned defense of the chair as deterrent may be read by a board member of the Civil Liberties Union, the exegesis of Bruce Springsteen by a man who thinks Beethoven a Bolshevik. But since it is the examiner's duty to cast aside prejudice, this is a minor problem.

The mangling of the English language, however, is not a minor problem. That in which one is interested is the "object," not the "subject" of one's interests. One can of course be interested in a subject— water polo, the paintings of Vermeer, grammar. That is "a subject which interests" one. If you want to say, "Write about a subject which interests you," say it. In the next edition of this application, for choice.

Injustice Witnessed:
ESSAYS ABOUT CRIMES *of* ALL SORTS

In a utopia, there would be no need for law—or lawyers. The law student's raison d'être is the existence of injustice. The desire for justice is the purest of motivations for the aspiring lawyer.

You may see injustice in an abstract, political form, as did Stephanie Cotsirilos, or you may even play a role, as Steven Lofchie found himself doing. Both of these writers are especially effective, because rather than prattling on with pretentious adjectives about motivations, they re-create scenes that thrust the reader into their experiences.

L. Roger Boord's essay, one of our favorites from the original edition of this book, takes an unflinching look at the consequences of literal lawlessness. Though his references are today outdated, his message is timeless.

In writing an essay like these, you can demonstrate your sensitivity to the world's imperfections and your sympathy to troubles beyond yourself. You show that you can be trusted to treat your law degree, and the knowledge and authority it represents, as more than a money machine.

STEPHANIE COTSIRILOS

Epidaurus

My mother and I arrived at the hills of Epidaurus in the early evening and walked up the old path to the theatre. Distant relatives lay in the countryside, their bones becoming part of the rock formation below the olive trees and the sand. We found our places in the stone amphitheatre, which broke at its edges into boulders. We had come to see Euripides' *Electra*. My mother crumpled a Kleenex, and the acoustics made it sound like a small hurricane in her hand.

The military junta was still in power in Greece that summer. In Athens, we had dined with a Greek couple, both liberal academics who loved to dance. The wife had become increasingly nervous as her husband made jokes about the government within earshot of the waiters. Years later, in New York, a young woman would relate to me her experience of the penalty this wife feared for her husband.

Now, at Epidaurus, junta elite entered the theatre. We watched the audience stand and applaud briefly, as required.

Dusk fell and the play began, repeating its ancient litany of personal betrayal and political struggle. Finally, Electra and Orestes stood silently at opposite ends of the stage, and the actors' moment of recognition spilled beyond the boundaries of the play. The performers' silence communicated, deliberately, defiance and a demand for liberty. So when brother and sister broke and ran into each other's arms, the theatre at Epidaurus exploded with the sound of Greeks on their feet, cheering and applauding around the seated, unsmiling military. This time, my mother and I applauded too. Many minutes passed before the actors would continue the play.

STEVEN LOFCHIE

Driving a Cab in New York City

Ateenager wearing a hooded sweatshirt opened my cab door. He and two friends piled into the back. A fourth man wanted to sit beside me. It was late and my wallet was so stuffed it wouldn't fold. I motioned him into the back. He asked, "You nervous to let me sit with you?" That he must challenge me was a rule of our game. He likely had a knife and might try to rob me if it seemed easy.

My riders gave as their destination the Red Hook projects, a complex of tall, ugly buildings near the elevated tracks in Brooklyn. I drove fast and erratically, throwing them about the backseat, keeping them uncomfortable. I watched them in the rearview mirror. Their conversation was too low for me to hear. We sped and jolted past the gutted buildings and the garbage-piled lots.

At our destination, I slammed both the gas and brake. Then I shifted into reverse. When the rear door opened, I released the brake. The cab raced backward. This was one of my standard defenses. "No one leaves before paying," I announced.

Crumpled money was pushed through the partition. Two riders burst out. I wouldn't let them near my window. The cab rolled forward and gained speed, two passengers caught inside. One banged his fist behind my head. The partition clattered. I slowed to twenty, slow enough for them to jump. One stumbled clumsily.

For six years, mostly part-time, I drove cabs. The job was a succession of threatening situations. When I was sufficiently careful, I did not learn if the threats had been real or imagined.

NAME WITHHELD

Michael Stewart was an inner-city "kid" who kept to himself, his mother remembers. He fancied himself an artist, and to this end, he drew subway art, even though this was illegal. One day while he was creating this outlawed form of expression, he was arrested by a policeman. From this point on the details as to what happened are somewhat obscure. What is known is that the would-be Picasso ended up in a coma with cuts and bruises all over his body. Two weeks later, Mrs. Stewart laid to rest her nineteen-year-old son.

There were several eyewitnesses to the events of the afternoon on which Michael Stewart was mortally wounded. Though the stories varied according to how much each person saw, the one constant thread in each was that he was beaten by policemen. Not just one or two policemen, but *ten* officers took part in "subduing" Stewart. "New York's Finest" explained their actions as necessary in controlling the suspect. They only used their nightsticks while it was necessary, after which they brought Stewart to jail. However, the same eyewitnesses concur that Stewart was in no way resisting the policemen. They beat him unmercifully in broad daylight, and his only real "crime" was being black in a white man's world.

The New York City District Attorney's office immediately and inexplicably cleared seven of the officers of any wrongdoing. The other three officers were ordered to stand trial. They were eventually found not guilty, after the coroner changed his story about the autopsy on three different occasions. Michael Stewart's death was ruled a suicide, although the evidence proved that he could not have beaten himself into a coma.

This is an example of the brand of justice that black Americans have come to expect. A jury of our peers still means a jury of our "overseers." The problem will only be righted by black people because it is for black people. Yet, black lawyers would rather go on to the large law firm which will pay him/her the "big money." This is the dilemma that will face me in a few short years. Sometimes I think that I cannot make a difference all by myself. But by becoming part of the system that condones and supports this kind of justice, I would be a part of the problem. I pray to God that I find a solution that I can live with, and still live with myself.

NAME WITHHELD

When I was twelve years old, I wanted to be the first woman president of the United States. Throughout high school, I prepared for this vocation; majoring in political science in college was an easy choice. Much to my surprise, though, political science led me to change my plans and abandon the race for the White House.

Elective office cannot be part of the American dream for everyone. Expensive political technologies such as media advertising and consulting make large campaign coffers necessary for competitive candidates. Moreover, because of money's role in elections, contributors have special access to politics and can exercise disproportionate influence in the decision-making process.

Summer experiences verified these conclusions. While an intern at Common Cause, a citizens' lobby group specializing in campaign finance, I saw that political action committees and wealthy contributors play a large role in the decision-making process. Subsequent internships with two senators evidenced how legislators frequently plan their strategies in an effort to appease monied interests.

Running for office has lost its appeal. Rather than destroying my dreams, though, disillusionment has pointed me in a new direction and has increased my desire to work towards electoral reform. Law school may tarnish more of my golden ideals. However, I have learned to look beyond my disappointments and look forward to the challenges that accompany them.

L. ROGER BOORD

T he law is rooted in history and philosophy. To fully understand the law, each person must make his own journey through those subjects and arrive at his own perceptions. In 1987, I attended the University of Cambridge, England, where I studied modern political thought and the history of World War II. The purpose of this essay is to show how my studies and my experiences traveling influenced my desire to work for human rights through the legal profession.

Amsterdam, The Netherlands. In a room hidden in the back of an office building on the Prisengracht Canal, I saw pasted on the walls a collection of pictures of Hollywood movie stars and European figures taken from magazines of the 1940s. This, and the scattered papers of a diary, were the only surviving remnants found of a young Jewish girl who had hidden in this secret annex until deported to Bergen-Belsen in 1944.

Even after forty years, the atrocities committed by the Nazi regime shock the civilized mind. The photographs of piles of mutilated corpses leave me in bewildering numbness, but seeing the Anne Frank house personalized the horror by applying a face, a soul to one of those victims. The experience raised the difficult question: Why was life taken from the innocent? I could only find the answer by understanding the process by which innocent life can become valueless.

West Berlin, Federal Republic of Germany. I saw West Berlin today as a bright metropolis reflecting a modern Germany prospering in the confidence of its own success. But the Germany of the young Adolf Hitler was engulfed in political and economic turmoil. The Weimer Republic seemed too burdened with parliamentary weaknesses to deal effectively with economic chaos and the growing threats of Soviet communism. Hitler offered a radical solution, but few fully comprehended his ominous words: "In the struggle between two philosophies, only can the weapon of brute force, persistently and ruthlessly applied, lead to a decision for the side it supports."

Within four weeks of his rise to Chancellor, Hitler abolished freedom of speech, press, assembly, and the laws against arbitrary search and seizure. This act formed the real basis for Nazi rule since it enabled the police to bypass the courts. As Goering put it, "The law and the will of the Fuhrer are one." Human rights and the rule of law had ceased to exist in Germany.

(East) Berlin, German Democratic Republic. Many Germans saw Hitler as a leader who could protect their nation from the domination of Soviet Communism. But because the Fuhrer put himself above the law, that fear became reality in a separate Germany. East Berlin is the European communist model of happiness and prosperity. To me it was like an amusement park, without amusement. Under the cold, colorless apartment buildings sagging with age and neglect, I saw Soviet soldiers stroll the streets. A colossal statue of Lenin looms ominously in the center of the city, not far from where parallel concrete walls separated by a 200-yard strip of death imprison a nation still deprived of the rule of law. As I surveyed this grim scene I reflected on the similarities in political reality between Hitler's race-socialism and Lenin's class-socialism.

In 1917, Lenin seized power from the Russian Provisional Government. He described his dictatorship as "the rule—unrestricted by law and based on force—of the proletariat over the bourgeoisie." The courts were replaced by revolutionary tribunals and Lenin's secret police. The purpose was to purge the nation of those people whom Lenin classified as "harmful insects"—i.e. to kill people collectively and not individually. As Cheka official M.Y. Latsis explained,

> *"We are not carrying out war against individuals. We are exterminating the bourgeoisie as a class. We are not looking for evidence or witnesses . . . The first question we ask is—to what class does he belong, what are his origins, upbringing, education or profession? These questions define the fate of accused."*

Munich, F.R.G. Hitler had indeed learned well from Soviet Russia. At the Nazi prison camp Dachau, I saw the grisly results of the abolition of law—prison cells for the untried, with the crematorium in efficient proximity. I realized that thousands suffered and died because Nazi ideology could not tolerate their living.

Here was the answer to my question—the diabolical process which sets rule of law aside, extinguishing the hopes and dreams of precious individuals like Anne Frank.

> *Sometimes it is said that man cannot be trusted with the government of himself. Can he, then, be trusted with the government of others? Let history answer this question.*
>
> *Thomas Jefferson*

Charlottesville, Virginia. I believe that the concepts of liberal democracy and the rule of law are founded first upon the belief in eternal moral principles which secure "self-evident" and "inalienable" rights to every human being; and secondly, on the philosophy that each individual is responsible for his own behavior, as well as morally obligated to live within the limitations posed by the rights of others. No circumstance of "class struggle," "racial preservation," or any assumed need to go "above the law" can justify abolishing these rights. Human beings can only be properly judged individually, and only through such judgment under the due process of law can a government legitimately take forcible action against any person.

But denial of human rights is still commonplace in 1987. When an enemy is perceived to be at a nation's throat, the tendency is, as Hitler put it, to meet lawlessness with equal lawlessness. But the question is: Can a nation's moral fiber be stretched to whatever shape seems expedient to preserve it?

We must remember that in essence, a nation is what it stands for, especially when standing for that something becomes most difficult. And the "somethings" for which the United States must first stand are justice, truth, and the value of every human being.

I wish to dedicate myself to promotion and protection of these principles. The essence of individual human rights is absolute and universal. That was as clear and essential to a fourteen-year-old Dutch girl in 1944 as it is to a twenty-one-year-old American college student in 1987, or it was to his school's founder in 1776.

I know what I want, I have a goal, an opinion, I have a religion and love. Let me be myself and then I am satisfied.

Anne Frank

Jugglers: ESSAYS ABOUT APPLICANTS *with* COLORFUL BACKGROUNDS

The variety of scenarios, cases, decisions, people, and ideas lawyers encounter attracts many people to the profession. Most law schools, meanwhile, are looking for a body of diverse students who can stimulate one another and bring a range of perspectives and experiences to the school.

One successful angle for an essay, then, is to show how much a Renaissance person you are. "A diverse class is a better class," one dean told us. "If I could have the perfect class, the only thing I can say for sure is that it would have three hundred seventy-five very different people."

Discussing how all of your activities, skills, and accomplishments fit together can show your work ethic, your versatility, and your passion. But no one wants to read a résumé posing as an essay. Explain how, for example, your love of music and your Texas background make you a more vivid, sensitive, driven, and/or exciting person. Interesting and telling detail is the key to effective writing. Show and explain—don't just prattle.

Jay Pomerantz describes how teaching, day care, and music have honed his business and legal skills. His résumé, which might seem flaky or directionless to a high-powered lawyer, is revealed to be an excellent preparation for law school. Pomerantz succeeds because he challenges the reader to think about familiar subjects in a new way and because he supports his assertions with concrete examples that are interesting and amusing.

In the next essay, Tyson Branyan avoids what he calls "Lincolnesque" statements, and as a result his piece is more readable and relevant than its length first suggests.

Branyan manages to pull off the "preemptive" essay. In discussing his career and his background, he addresses potential objections before they can be raised. While he admits that his experiences may not be deep, he argues that a law education offers the chance to become a "specialist." Though he is only one-eighth Choctaw, he designated American Indian as his background and argues that he "felt" Indian growing up. Merely by showing that he has thought about these shadows, Branyan melts their damage and even turns them to his advantage.

Jamil Jaffer's family has also made an interesting journey, and Jaffer uses that background to present himself and his well-considered goals for law school. He has clearly determined a niche for himself. His essay has confidence without arrogance—an appealing tone.

JAY POMERANTZ

I have just finished three active and concurrent career explorations. They consist of directing an after-school day care, teaching at the University of California at Santa Cruz, and working as a musician. Each job has challenged my ability to communicate effectively, to think precisely while under pressure, and to organize a large number of details. All require creative decision making. These work experiences have been invaluable; coinciding with the self-exploration of my twenties, they have served as extended and comprehensive aptitude tests. I have pinpointed the kinds of activities I enjoy, and those in which I excel. My personal statement is devoted to outlining these activities, and to discussing how they led me to the conclusion that I should pursue a career in law.

Directing a day care demands the ability to do many things well—almost at once. It is common that in a single five-minute period, I have to deal with: (1) two children who have just trashed the school bathroom; (2) another who has just discovered lice in her hair; (3) a boy crying because his teacher confiscated a toy; (4) a parent demanding to review the billing records; (5) a mother on the phone asking me not to allow her ex-boyfriend to pick up her child; (6) an aide who cannot find the right project supplies; and (7) a kid hopping the fence. To survive, I have learned patience, the ability to recall a large number of small but important details, and how to delegate responsibility.

My six years in day care have honed my communication skills and have introduced me to the world of business management. Children can be demanding, irrational, cunning, and obstinate in ways that adults often never imagine. While it may seem routine to an outsider, the task of convincing a recalcitrant six-year-old to pick up the Legos he just scattered across the room requires negotiating skills of the highest level. A day does not go by when some complicated compromise is not reached to guarantee that a child will comply with the rules without losing faith. (The concepts of fairness and the organic development of a body of laws are ever present.) Likewise, daily contact with the parents and guardians of over 90 children has taught me to choose my words with precision and care. As director, I am responsible for an annual budget of over $100,000, the hiring, training, and supervision of a staff of five, the purchase of all supplies, and the monthly billing. The fact that the program has more than doubled in size over the last three years has greatly increased the level of these activities. I found that I like managing both people and money; career conversations with attorneys have confirmed that these skills figure prominently in the practice of law.

Music is an enduring and compelling interest. Business skills have enabled me to translate that interest into a wide range of musical activity. I have successfully enlisted the support of professional studios in the recording of my own material, resulting in a full-length album that I co-produced, packaged, and distributed. Club owners and booking agents are some of the most irascible people on the planet, but I have learned to deal with them effectively. My band performs regularly at local clubs. A publishing company offered me a contract for several songs. An eye-opening meeting with a music lawyer in Monterey demonstrated the complexity of entering into such agreements. It also demonstrated the potential for combining music and law in a legal career. I strongly believe that different careers and interests can be integrated; they need not be mutually exclusive. I intend to practice law with this in mind.

It was my involvement with music that sparked a passion for all the arts. My undergraduate degree in Art History led directly to an appointment as a university teaching assistant. This, in turn, resulted in my current job as Visiting Lecturer at the University of California at Santa Cruz. This fall marks the fourth year that I have been one of the instructors for the Core Course, an interdisciplinary class for first-year students. The course uses the study of the arts to introduce the students to new modes of thinking and writing. Small tutorials are the primary teaching unit. I have planned and led these tutorials, given lectures on a wide range of topics, written all my course assignments, commented on student essays, and written the Student Narrative Evaluations.

Frankly, I feel that I have learned all I can as day care director *cum* university teacher. Life and lessons in both arenas are recycling. I am now thirty. My cognitive self demands new direction and a longer-range sense of purpose. It is this voice that has lobbied for the examination of law as a career.

To this end, I made a set of systematic career investigations. First, I consulted with the law advisor at UC Santa Cruz. Next, I arranged a half dozen interviews with practicing attorneys. These interviews left me with a detailed, unidealized notion of what it means to work as an attorney; they supported my assumption that what I have learned since graduation will serve me well in the field. And finally, I attended a number of law classes. My interest in the material confirmed my decision to attend law school. Any concern I had about making the jump into this competitive field, with its fair share of difficult people, evaporated when one of my lawyer/day care parents refused to switch jobs with me for the day—he feared he could not handle the intensity of the day care.

In the introduction to the standard application, the notion that a lawyer must confront a diverse set of challenges is stressed. I have enclosed the album I co-wrote and produced as evidence of my ability to do just that. The making of this required the necessary music and organizational skills, a fluency in computer language in the application of MIDI and SMPTE, graphics and advertising skills, as well as the overriding ability to make decisions, to solve problems, and to see something through to its completion.

TYSON BRANYAN

If the Committee has waded through my academic/work history, it should be clear that I've done a great many different things. To keep that history to a manageable length, I've left out many details as to responsibilities and items learned along the way. You will just have to read between the lines and accept that much useful knowledge was acquired and useful skills honed. I didn't even discuss avocational areas, such as the weekends I spent roadracing motorcycles at tracks all over California or the fact that my job enabled me to pilot a small plane over most of the western United States. I've done geological work in Alaska and have traveled extensively in Europe and Great Britain. I'm still a competitive athlete and often coach youth sports. I've worked very hard, but I've also had some fun. I've enjoyed my work and the small financial rewards it has brought with it.

There is one thing however, that I have not enjoyed. That is that I've always been a generalist. The Committee can deduce this. I went from Geol/Engnr to Soc/Anthro and back again. I've done a wide variety of jobs, each with wide responsibilities. Though a partner in TYDECO, I've basically been self-employed these past four years. It suits me well and keeps me sharp to have this variety, but it is difficult to be continually climbing the learning curve. There are no classes offered anywhere entitled "Uranium Exploration 101" or "How to Get a Good Deal from Major Oil Companies." I'm basically self-taught in the "South Texas School of Hard Knocks," and in most cases this has been more than adequate, if expensive at times.

However, self-taught has no place in the world of laws. I've had to constantly defer to others as to technicalities and implications of rules, regulations, contracts and agency jurisdictions. I've had both good and bad experiences with retained counsel throughout the years. In the back of my mind though, there always ran two strains of emotion: first a feeling of being at a disadvantage because of my ignorance, and second, a little jealousy that this person was dealing with very interesting issues that I liked and for which I had a good feel. Last year the final straw came when I was involved with the purchase of a tungsten mill in Nederland, Colorado. By the time we had wrangled through the legal complexities of an 1880s' water right, centered in the Denver watershed, I knew my future lay in a career in law.

The experience with the water right convinced me that I would enjoy and succeed in a career in law, and that I should pursue this long postponed goal. Without much guidance, I found out how to register with LSDAS and took the LSAT this past December. My score of 41 is not stunning, but will insure that I have a good chance to be accepted at the schools to which I've applied here in the Southwest.

Frankly, I never considered applying to Cornell until February 1st. It was then that I received the letter that is sent to certain LSDAS Referral Service Candidates. This letter he outlined some of Cornell's assets and just as importantly, waived the February 1st application deadline for recipients of that letter. Because of this correspondence I was motivated to speak to friends and others who are familiar with your institution and with Ithaca. I also spoke with your admissions office, a recent Cornell Law graduate, and your American Indian law students' representative. I wanted to be sure that Cornell was truly interested in a diverse student population.

Mr. Stearns and I discussed many aspects of my background and how it related to the admissions process at Cornell. Evidently, I received the Dean's letter because I had marked that I was Native American when registering with LSDAS. I related that I am "only" an eighth or sixteenth Choctaw by blood and, because it is so patently self-serving, I have very mixed feelings about even mentioning it during the admissions process. In no way have I ever been disadvantaged due to my Choctaw heritage. On the other hand, after a lifetime of being proud of this heritage and being especially close to my Grandmother Nona, I wasn't about to deny it now. It aggravates me to discuss (defend?) my "Indianness" as I'm doing here, but Mr. Stearns and others assured me that your admissions committee would be interested in hearing some of what I related to him.

My grandmother was born Nona Mae Collins at the turn of the century in Indian Territory. For governmental purposes she was classified as ¼ Choctaw. She lived in a small settlement named Ti, I.T., and was later sent to the Choctaw boarding schools for girls in Tuskahoma. Typically, speaking Choctaw was forbidden here, as assimilation was the order of the day. In most respects, assimilation worked well for her, as it did for most individual Choctaws. She got a job in the Oklahoma City stockyards, married a cowboy and had three daughters. Two of these daughters married Indian; my mother did not. It was a shock to me to finally realize that I was "less Indian" than my cousins, but nonetheless, we were all equally part of a grand matrilineal family, dominated by one very special Choctaw woman; a woman who entertained us with her stories and invigorated us with her love. Today Nona is an old, frail, yet still elegant woman who is pleased with her life and her family.

There's more that I could say about all of this; but I'm not, because my homelife was what I considered normal middle class. I grew up in Cushing, Oklahoma, a town of 6,500 that I mistakenly thought was a city. I was in high school when my family moved to Southern California, and I quickly learned that Cushing wasn't much of a place. I was at no disadvantage though and did well in California schools and graduated from Chapman College with honors. As my work history shows, I've had success in business and life in general. I'm happily married and now have two children, age 4 and 2.

I've written my life story in this statement partly to respond to Item No. 6 on your admissions application and also because Cornell seems genuinely interested in the total candidate. I've applied to several other schools to which my statements could only be described as "terse," because I feel my resume, my academic career and my LSAT scores can speak for themselves. I'm sure I would not have written this much for Cornell if I had applied prior to February 1st and had I not received the Dean's letter. This despite being advised that Ivy League schools particularly like statements that are "Lincolnesque." I've resisted this while trying to just sketch in the facts.

I would like to attend Cornell because of what I now believe I know about it. The school turns out competent people who are not limited as to where or what they can practice. It is evidently challenging and interesting, and I'd be disappointed if Cornell wasn't difficult. Importantly, Ithaca seems like a place my family would find comfortable for a few years. Cornell also offers a chance to study Indian law and that is one of my personal measures for an acceptable law school. Though I am only going to attend a school that offers this possibility, what I'll do with it I refuse to speculate. The Indians I know are like anybody else—they need competent counsel for rather ordinary situations. If Cornell wants students with certain backgrounds in order to round out its official ethnic population, I'm not sure I'm the candidate for you. If the slot I am seeking is reserved only for disadvantaged Indian students, it would be a disservice to several parties to offer it to me. On the other hand, if Cornell truly wants people who have diverse backgrounds and who will be a credit to the University after graduation, I do feel I have the qualifications for which you are looking and believe my attendance at Cornell might work out well for all of us.

NAME WITHHELD

During the previous four years I have been employed as Principal at a high school in Illinois. The school was a boarding school for students gifted in dance and/or music. My duties included the coordination of all programs offered; presentations to the board of directors; development, supervision, and evaluation of all academic faculty; course and curriculum development; student advisement and placement; implementation of the budget; designing master schedules for faculty and students; development of all school handbooks; and supervision of all extracurricular organizations and student activities.

Before coming to the school, I was employed as a social studies teacher at a junior high school. I was responsible for developing the curriculum as well as working on the budget and ordering materials. I also served as Assistant Gifted Coordinator; assisted the Student Council; served as a member of the parent/teacher committee; coached track; and was responsible for a variety of after-school activities involving students from grades K through 8.

I have been successful in a variety of situations dealing with diverse groups of people. I was responsible for managing a family-owned grocery store in Illinois. I worked with various minorities as a Youth Supervisor in the Illinois area. I taught many Amish students during my stay in Arcola and I was associated with world-renowned artists as well as an international student body at my high school. I believe these successful experiences illustrate that I possess the interpersonal skills as well as the integrity, energy, and determination required by a career in law.

I believe that my membership in Kappa Delta Pi and Phi Delta Kappa along with my success in graduate school to be a more accurate reflection of my academic potential than my undergraduate work. I am eager and anxious to apply my academic and professional experiences at the Indiana University School of Law and I am confident that my addition to the student body would be a positive and productive one for both myself and the school.

JAMIL JAFFER

I come from a family of pioneers. We are not the kind of pioneers that traversed the American landscape in search of their fortune in the Wild West. Rather, I come from a family whose path began in the sweltering heat of India, crossed a vast ocean to the shores of East Africa, passed through the frigid climes of Canada, and ended in the sunshine of Southern California. My own personal journey has led me through many of these same locales and further—all the way to our nation's capital.

My great-grandfather was an adventurous man. When the offer came to leave his homeland of India to travel to British East Africa, he jumped at the opportunity. He left his family and friends behind and boarded a ship bound for Tanzania with only the clothes he could fit into a burlap sack and some money his family had gathered together at the last minute. It was this same adventurous spirit that took hold of me toward the end of my college career, when I decided to move across the nation to Washington, D.C. Raised on a steady diet of National Public Radio and history books from the "discard" pile at the library, I always knew that I wanted to study the law. As a child, I was the kid who took my father's portable radio to school in the fifth grade so that I could listen to the Iran-Contra hearings.

I considered applying directly to law school after graduating from UCLA. But after a period of self-examination, I realized that while my education at UCLA was excellent, it was not connected to the world outside. I wanted some practical experience and decided to seek my fortune in the District of Columbia. Leaving my family behind, I came to Washington without a job or a place to live, only with a burning desire to become a part of the American political process. Like my father, who came to Canada in 1969 with nothing but a few hundred dollars in his wallet and the name of an uncle he could stay with, I was looking for a place to call home.

With some effort and not a little bit of luck, I found a job on Capitol Hill working with computers, using some of the same skills that helped me pay my way through four years of college. Being so close to the political process, I began to hunger for legislative work. Within a few months, I was given legislative responsibility in defense, foreign affairs, trade and science policy. Combining these diverse areas with my technological background, I have begun to study the rapidly developing field of technology law.

My primary interest in this arena deals with intellectual property law. Recent court cases have supported the notion that an innovative business process may be patentable. Given the rapid pace of invention that is critical to the high-tech economy, such patents could potentially create a substantial barrier to competition. The expansion of the Internet into the world of commerce has created new challenges in protecting intellectual property without inhibiting the free market. Business process patents appear to have the effect of granting a government enforced monopoly over a vast range of technological and entrepreneurial processes. The threat of costly patent litigation alone could limit many investors from directing capital into new technologies. Some scholars argue that business process patents serve to protect all inventors, large and small alike. Such a position is tenable only when inventors have the resources and wherewithal to enforce their patents and to defend against competing claims. Given the large market capitalizations of established companies in this sector and their corresponding ability to bring substantial resources to bear on potential litigation, smaller inventors may have a difficult time raising the venture capital that has driven the rapid growth of the technology industry in recent years. It is important that Congress examine the patent laws to determine what beneficial or adverse effects these laws may have on the new information economy.

In working with technology issues and the development of innovative ideas, my interest in national security led me to consider the issue of cybersecurity. Cybersecurity raises the question of how these new ideas are protected while they reside on a global computer network. Information security goes directly to the question of whether the users of the Internet are able to rely on a secure and robust communications infrastructure. If consumers and businesses cannot be assured that their information will be protected, it is unlikely that the information economy will continue to grow at its current pace. This is a policy arena that crosses typical boundaries of law and policy, and raises issues of international law, national security policy, antitrust law and public-private sector relations. In this realm, it is important that the government consider the issues of infrastructure protection and information security education, while working closely with the private sector to bring its working expertise to bear on this important arena.

Many of these issues transcend traditional frameworks of political and academic organization. Having seen the process of lawmaking from the inside, I am ready to begin my study of the law and its interpretation. I come from a family committed to education, one that has instilled in me a strong work ethic. At the same time, I am the first of my family to attempt a law school education and the first to seek a career in public service. For me, law school is akin to the boat that my great-grandfather sailed to a new future—it is my passage to a pioneering adventure, studying the evolving intersection between technology and the law. I feel that the University of Chicago Law School will provide me with the opportunity to explore this largely uncharted field.

NAME WITHHELD

O ne may ask, "Why would a psychology major be interested in a legal career?" Of all the questions that have been broached concerning my plans to enter law school, this one most frequently occurs. In my opinion there are natural links between law and psychology due to the fact that they are both human services. My interest in human problems and interpersonal communication, which led me to pursue psychology, now motivates my pursuit of law. Law epitomizes these attractions in psychology as well as encourages analytical thought processes, rational problem-solving, and defining a concrete legal methodology for solutions.

Law began to seriously interest me last year while I was working as an adolescent counselor in a psychiatric hospital. In daily counseling situations I was given opportunity to utilize my listening, analytical, and rational skills. I learned that active listening to both the words verbalized and the feelings left submerged was difficult. A vital component of successful treatment, I realized, was interpersonal communication. In counseling situations I also incorporated both analytical and rational thought processes to develop a diagnosis of the patient's problem. Interacting with people in this manner truly challenged me while solidifying my determination to enter a people-helping profession.

Psychology helps people deal with their mental and emotional problems. After considering not only my desire to help people but

interpersonal and analytical aptitudes, I concluded that my
e is to serve people in a more comprehensive way. Law serves as
umbrella under which problems ranging from corporate disagreements to personal claims are resolved. Although I desire to utilize the interpersonal skills gained by my training in psychology, I am also attracted by the analytical aspects of law. Inherent within law are opportunities to exercise my altruistic characteristics and satisfy my desire to develop definite analytical solutions. I believe my proficiency in psychology enhanced by my personal experiences enables me to enter the field of law with unique advantages.

ESSAY *News*

───────

ESSAY *Advice*

───────

ESSAY *Reviews*

───────

ESSAY *Help*

www.essaysthatworked.com